She Cheated

Recovering Your Heart and Life After Her Affair

Bryce Jackson

Legal Disclaimer

This book is intended to provide general information only. Neither the author nor publisher provides any legal or other professional advice. If you need professional advice, you should seek advice from the appropriate licensed professional. This book does not provide complete information on the subject matter covered. This book is not intended to address specific requirements, either for an individual or an organization. This book is intended to be used only as a general guide and not as a sole source of information on the subject matter. While the author has undertaken diligent efforts to ensure accuracy, there is no guarantee of accuracy or of no errors, omissions or typographical errors. Any slights of people or organizations are unintentional. The author and publisher shall have no liability or responsibility to any person or entity and hereby disclaim all liability, including without limitation, liability for consequential damages regarding any claim, loss or damage that may be incurred, or alleged to have been incurred, directly or indirectly, arising out of the information provided in this book.

Published by: Bryce Jackson
ISBN: 978-1-7347743-0-6

All biblical references NASB unless otherwise stated.

Table of Contents

Dedicated to My Band of Brothers

Preface

This book was born out of frustration. Discovering that my wife was having an affair devastated me. I didn't know what to do. I wanted to save my marriage, but I couldn't find any resources to help me out.

I tried to find some books on the subject. The ones I found were about reforming men who had cheated on their wives; surely, someone else whose wife had cheated on them had written a book.

To make matters worse, I knew plenty of guys who had cheated on their wives, but I didn't know any whose wives had cheated on them. Since then, I have learned that many men have been down this road; they just don't talk about it publicly.

If you find yourself dealing with an unfaithful wife, my heart goes out to you. I'm not sure if there is anything that a man goes through that can be harder than this. The intense pain of her infidelity is magnified by a deep sense of emasculation.

I hope this book will be helpful to you. It is honest and raw, and comes from the lessons learned in my journey.

If you are a friend to a man whose wife has cheated on him, I hope this book will give you insight into the pain he is going through and will help you be a better friend. When something like this happens, sometimes it's hard to know what to say. That's okay; just be there for your friend.

Finally, if you are a counselor, pastor, or leader at a church, thank you for reading this book. Infidelity by women seems to be increasing. While I know that a primary role of the Church is to keep marriages together, when things do go wrong, you need to know how to love and lead the men under your care. I hope this book gives insight into the heart of a man devastated by his wife's infidelity.

I am not a counselor or an ordained minister, and the ideas in this book are not from a classroom. I am simply a man who went through one of the darkest valleys that he can go through with God and emerged on the other side alive.

Thank God for my Band of Brothers, a ragtag group of men who got gut-level honest with each other one night and have walked together now for nearly ten years. Thank you to the Sage for his calm wisdom. Thank you to Tom for his fatherly advice. Major "thank yous" to my counselor who challenged me to see things from a different perspective.

I also owe a deep debt to the authors who stretched me during this season. Gerald May's *The Awakened Heart* challenged me to stay present even in my pain. John Eldredge's *Journey of Desire* helped me dream of a better future. *Surrender to Love* by David Benner helped me see the love of God. *I Told Me So* by Gregg Ten Elshof revealed my tremendous capacity for self-deception. *Shattered Dreams* by Larry Crabb led me through the path of disappointment to a brighter future that now allows me to help you.

Writing a book out of the pain of my own life is tough, especially when the story involves more people than just me. Therefore, I've decided to publish this book under a pseudonym to protect the dignity of my children, their mother, and the men who have courageously shared stories with me.

Finally, thank you for purchasing this book. The profits go to worthy organizations that help men navigate the pain of infidelity and recover their hearts as men.

Introduction

My phone rang at 5:45 a.m. I was in the back of a taxi, riding to catch a flight home from Las Vegas. That week I'd been working at a trade show. Exhausted, I was looking forward to getting home.

After three long days of talking with people at the trade show booth, leading training sessions, and entertaining clients, I was dead tired. The night before, I had collapsed in my hotel bed, looking for some much-needed rest. Sleep wouldn't come, though, and I tossed and turned all night. Something was wrong; I was about to find out what it was. Little did I know that a journey had already started and it would change my life forever.

Early the following morning, I gathered my belongings and hailed a taxi back to the airport. As I sat in the back seat driving through the darkness, my cell phone rang.

On the other end of the line, my wife of 16 years was in tears. Why was she calling me so early? She sounded hysterical.

"I'm so sorry," she said. "I didn't mean for it to happen and it won't happen again."

"What won't happen again?"

"After school yesterday, Jim came over to pick up something. I invited him to stay for dinner."

My wife was a college teacher. Jim was a former adult student who we had gotten to know. He was struggling with post-traumatic stress disorder from the Iraq War and on a path to giving his life to God. He'd been in the small group we hosted at our home. My wife had counseled him and his girlfriend. I had spent time with him talking about life and God.

"You did what?"

"He stayed for dinner. Then we started watching a movie."

My blood pressure was rising quickly. "You let him stay for a movie? With

our son there?"

"He fell asleep during the second movie and left later that evening. Nothing happened, I swear."

As I sat slouched in the back of that taxicab, it was as if a bomb had been dropped in my heart. Dazed and confused, I stumbled into the airport through security and into the plane seat. Staring out the window for the next three hours, my mind raced as I tried to make sense of the news.

Common Threads

Every man whose wife has cheated on him has a unique story. The details are always different. Regardless, however, all men who have experienced the infidelity of a cheating wife share some things in common:

We know the searing pain of a deeply wounded heart.

We know the disorientation of finding out that things are not what they seem.

We know the new-found discovery of tears.

We know new types of anger.

We know the desperation to return things to the way they were.

Most of all, we know the deep emasculation that happens when our wife chooses another man over us.

You didn't choose this path or plan on this. Yet, you've been thrown headfirst into a battle of epic proportions. It's a battle for your heart, for your children's hearts, and for your marriage.

The stakes couldn't be higher. It's like getting thrust into an MMA cage fight with a knife in your back, the wind knocked out of you, and you're battling for your life.

The next season of your life will call things out of you as a man that you didn't know existed. You'll feel emotions that you didn't know you could feel. You'll experience pain that you wouldn't wish on your worst enemy. All of this will be done in an environment of financial stress. To top it off, you'll need to be there for your kids who are even more confused and hurt than you are.

You're Not Alone

Sadly, you're not the first man to experience the trauma of an unfaithful wife. However, since most men don't like to talk about this subject, being in your situation can feel very lonely.

You are not alone. If you doubt me, just review the statistics: 13% of women admit to being unfaithful. (Institute for Family Studies, 2018) Given the reality that women who cheat have developed great skills at lying, I suspect this percentage is much higher.

Take heart. Many men have walked the path upon which you now find yourself. Throughout this book, you'll hear their stories, including their positive and negative responses to the situation.

There is Hope

A few months after I was thrust into the mess of my wife's infidelity, I shared a cup of coffee with a friend. He confided in me that his first wife had cheated on him. After some good words of advice, he looked at me and said something that made me want to punch his face: "You're going to be a better man on the other side of this."

At the time, this just made me angry. I didn't want to be a better man; I just wanted my marriage back. I wanted to escape the drowning sea of pain and return to normal.

Looking back ten years later, I can say that my friend was right. I've become a better man. In some strange way, I'm thankful for what I had to go through.

Here's the challenge: the promise of becoming a better man is not a guarantee. I've seen many men go off the deep end, making life choices that damaged themselves and their children. I've seen men harbor bitterness, allowing the pain to reshape their identity. I've seen men stuff the pain deep into their heart. Decades later, their lives are still off-track, impacted by the wounds of the affair. Trying to recapture some sense of normal, I've seen men push forward into multiple failed relationships or marriages. I've seen men's careers collapse.

Jonathan Martin says it well: "The waters that drown are the waters that save."[2] You don't have to drown. You can survive this season and emerge as a new man with a thriving life.

It will take courage and work to go on this journey. I will challenge you to ask yourself some hard questions. You will cry, but you will also be inspired to dream for your future at a time when dreaming feels more painful than ever.

Overview

The book is written in four phases. Consider each section a field guide for the stages you'll walk through.

Phase 1 is titled "Welcome to the Twilight Zone." In this section, we'll explore the realities of what just happened. This includes the emotional implications of where you find yourself.

Phase 2, "Recovering Your Heart," explores how your wife's choice to cheat impacted you as a man. Together, we'll seek healing and restoration.

Phase 3 is called "The Fight," and addresses how to battle for your marriage and family. Based on real-world input of what's going on in her heart, the practical advice offered in this section may be much different than what you think.

Phase 4 is titled "Your Next Chapter," and deals with loving your children during this crisis, and, finally, learning to forgive.

Take your time through each of these sections. My hope is that you will find healing for your heart, guidance for your journey, and encouragement for the fight. In all of this, I pray that you will discover the closeness of God and the friendship of other men. Most of all, I pray that through the fire, you will become a better man.

Phase 1: Welcome to the Twilight Zone

She cheated.

Everything that you once accepted as reality now has changed. The apple cart has been overturned. You're confused, your heart is broken, and you're jealous. To top it all off, your anger feels like it may consume you.

Welcome to the Twilight Zone. You have been unwillingly thrust into a new world. So many things that were once settled in your life are now up in the air:

Love: What happened? I thought she loved me. What about the vows? I knew our marriage wasn't perfect, but I had no idea she would choose another man over me. What did I do wrong? What do I need to change?

Family: What about our kids? This is so unfair to them. What will happen to them if we get divorced? How do I love them when my heart is crushed?

Finances: She's gone. How will I cover all the bills myself? What about our savings? Who will pay the debt? What happens if we get separated or divorced?

Friends: Who's on my side? Who's on her side? Right now, who cares—I don't want to see anybody, but I know I need people.

Much like you'd never choose a car wreck or a hurricane, you didn't choose this. The reality, though, is that it happened, and you are forced to live inside this confusing new world.

The first section of this book addresses the disorienting feelings of the Twilight Zone. If you've just discovered that your wife has cheated, then this will be helpful. If her affair happened a while back, I encourage you not to skip this section. It will help to revisit this time in your life to understand the emotions that shaped who you are today.

1: Shock

Some dates get etched into your mind. These are the times that change your life forever.

May 17 at 8:23 a.m. is one of these dates for me. This was about two and a half months after that Las Vegas phone call when my wife had told me that Jim had stayed for dinner and a movie. After that incident, she apologized and said that she was wrong. She had agreed to seek counseling once school dismissed for the summer. I thought everything was fine. I was about to learn otherwise.

Sitting in my home office on a Monday morning, my gut told me something wasn't right. The evening before had been strange. I was up late working on a project with some software developers in Europe and India. That evening while I was on the conference call, my wife came in, obviously shaken up. I was about to discover the beginning of her web of lies.

The previous Friday night, she had gone out with a group of girlfriends to celebrate a huge achievement in her career. Wanting her to have a good time and be safe, I encouraged her to stay at the hotel where they were going to hang out and see a band.

That evening when she left the house, she looked stunning. Her hair was curled and she was wearing a hot new outfit with new designer jeans. In the months before, she had been dieting and exercising consistently. For someone in her mid-thirties, she could have easily passed for a college undergrad.

She had come home midday on Saturday and we had spent the rest of the weekend together, doing what we usually do: hanging out, going to church, and working around the house. Little did I know that this would be the last time I would enjoy a normal weekend with her.

That Sunday night, she walked into my home office, visibly shaken. The web of lies was about to begin. Talking about the guy we had counseled, she said, "Jim's girlfriend is crazy." Having seen on Facebook that my wife was out on Friday night, she said Jim's girlfriend had concocted a story that my wife had met Jim and spent the night with her. At least this was a story I was likely to hear because of her jealousy.

After the incident two and a half months earlier when Jim had come over to our house, I thought our relationship was good. She assured me that she realized the relationship with Jim was inappropriate and had cut it off. Since then, she had taken steps in a positive direction. She had been to a women's weekend retreat in Colorado. We had shared an already-planned vacation together in Mexico. While I was concerned about her new drinking habit, she had assured me that when school was out, she would seek counseling over the summer.

Even though there were likely some obvious signs that I was ignoring out of my chosen naiveté, things seemed to be going well. I was holding out for summer so she could be restored in counseling. Summer was about to begin, so I was optimistic.

Before we went to bed that Sunday night, I prayed for her, asking God to give her peace and protect her from the "lies" that were being spread about her character. From there, we tried to go to sleep, but the night was restless.

In my office the next morning, I shared the story with my best friend who is a little less naive than me. "I hate to say this," he said, "but her story doesn't add up."

While we were on the phone, suspicion rose in my heart. I logged into our mobile phone account and for the first time ever looked at the call log.

My heart sank. Sure enough, there was a local number that appeared several times late Friday night and over the weekend.

You know the panicked feeling that invades your heart like a surge of hot adrenaline when you discover your wife has been with another man? Your mind starts racing, trying to put the pieces together. Anger begins to rise, combined with sadness and confusion.

Jumping in the car, I sped over to confront her in the parking lot of the building where she worked. Small fragments of the truth emerged, but the web of lies became thicker as the story changed.

The details continued to get worse. That previous Friday, she did in fact celebrate the promotion with her friends. Later that evening, though, after her friends had left, a prearranged rendezvous with Jim had happened in the hotel room I had reserved for her. She admitted it. There it was: my wife had committed adultery with another man.

In war, they talk about shell shock. It's a feeling of total disorientation after a bomb goes off. Your senses are overwhelmed, your ears ring, and your veins course with adrenaline. Your mind is fully alert, but at the same time you're immobilized.

My emotions revved to hyperdrive, yet at the same time I felt numb. Sadness and anger swirled with complete disbelief. My mind tried to get hold of the reality, but reality seemed like the beginning of a made-for-TV movie. How was this my life?

Take a Deep Breath

Not long before all of this happened, I had purchased an old sailboat. Having bought a never-ending fix-up project and getaway like this proved to be a huge gift during this season. Hours were spent floating around on the lake trying to clear my head.

As with most boats I have owned over the years, the soundtrack always included healthy doses of Jimmy Buffet. One of his more obscure songs was penned after Hurricane Katrina destroyed the lives of many New Orleans natives. The song is called "Breathe In, Breathe Out, Move On". The song's title says it all. Sometimes after a storm, you just need to take a deep breath and keep moving forward.

Your wife's betrayal feels like the aftermath of a huge storm. You didn't expect this to happen. Maybe it happened suddenly, or it crept up like the rising water of a flood, as it did for me. Maybe this isn't the first time she has cheated and your heart has been battered for a long time. In any case, much has been destroyed and you are in shock.

In this moment, nothing seems real. Your heart is reeling, and things that you took for granted are gone. What do you do now?

Right now, there isn't a whole lot you can do. You'll be learning that many things you thought you could control are things you actually have no control over at all. The best thing you can do is surrender to the moment and breathe.

The truth is that control is an illusion (not just in times of crisis, but in life in general). So, the faster you surrender yourself into the hands of a loving Father, the sooner he can start cleaning up the mess that's been made of your heart, emotions, and mind.

Your mind is frantic; you lie awake running through situations and scenarios, trying to figure out what went wrong and how to fix it. The best thing you can do is take a deep breath.

Your emotions are on high alert, surging with adrenaline. Sometimes, you throb with pain and sadness; other times, anger courses through your veins. The best thing you can do is breathe.

Sometimes, you are exhausted and numb. The intense emotions, combined with the lack of sleep and poor eating habits, take their toll. You find yourself staring blankly into space. This is a good time to just breathe.

Your New Reality

The biggest challenge right now is accepting your new reality. As surprising, infuriating, hurtful, and surreal as this is, it is happening to you. Here are some hard truths:

You have been violated. Your wife has chosen another man over you. This will forever impact your life.

Nobody wants to be in your situation. You didn't choose this, but it happened. Infidelity is now part of your story. She cheated, and you are affected.

A new chapter of your life has unfolded. As you process this reality, I want you to know two more (hopeful) things:

You are not alone.

This does not have to define the rest of your life.

Sadly, many men have been down this road before you. You may not know of any in your circle of friends—yet. However, you will soon discover that though no man wants to talk about it, many have walked through this valley of suffering.

While this is part of your story, it's important to remember that this is only one chapter in it. It does not have to define you forever.

Inviting God into Your New Reality

How will you get through this next season of your life? Right now, you don't need religious principles or shallow consolation. You need God, your Father, to be present with you.

It doesn't matter what your relationship with God has looked like up to this point. You may already have a close relationship with God or, in your pain, you may have cried out to him for the first time in a long time. Either way, he is there and willing to walk through this valley with you.

At the beginning of his ministry, Jesus walks to the front of his local synagogue and unrolls the scroll of Isaiah. He lands on a verse in Isaiah 61 that clearly explains his mission:

The Spirit of the Sovereign Lord is upon me because he has anointed me to preach good news to the poor, to bind up the brokenhearted, and to set the captives free.

You are brokenhearted. The good news is that Jesus has come for you.

I encourage you to pour your heart out to him. Let him know how your heart is broken. Tell him how confused and disoriented you are. Invite him into your heart to heal. Ask for his guidance.

2: Surrender

She moved out on Memorial Day weekend, less than two weeks after I found out. That Saturday, I had to get out of town. The first two hours of the five-hour drive were excruciating as I struggled to suppress tears with my five-year-old son in the back seat. He was going to spend the weekend at his grandparents.

After dropping him off, the flood gates opened up. For the next three hours, tears streamed down my face as I drove down the freeway. An overwhelming flow of emotions surged through my heart. Pain and anger swirled with deep sadness and confusion.

A few hours later, I found myself sitting on the couch of another older mentor that my friends affectionately call, "The Sage." I'll never forget his calm eyes as he listened.

After hearing my story, he quietly asked, "Are you ready to give her to God?"

"Excuse me?"

"Are you ready to give her to God?"

I'd never thought of this before. It sounded like the right thing to do, but what did that mean? She was my wife. Weren't we supposed to be one? Why would I give her away?

The truth is that much of my identity as a man was wrapped up in her and in our marriage. For most of my adult life, all I knew was her. My self-esteem was driven by her love for me, or lack thereof. My identity was as her husband and as a good family man.

Ever since we had first met and fallen in love, I had been going to her for answers to my two biggest questions. According to John Eldredge, author of *Wild at Heart*, every man has two fundamental questions: Am I loved, and, do I have what it takes? For almost 20 years, I had looked to my wife for the answers to these questions. She had provided love, and she had been the source of respect.

Now I found myself without her love and without the answers to these questions. If she cheated and lied, she certainly didn't respect me. I was lost. The wound she had delivered in choosing another man told me that not only was I not loved, but that I didn't have what it takes.

"Are you willing to give her to God?" asked the Sage again in a quiet voice.

When someone or something gives you that much of your identity, you tend to be very possessive or controlling of it. This amps up to the next level when it is taken away. These emotions are very revealing. They showed me that I was going to her for my source of life. In reality, what I was doing was going to her to get strength, rather than bringing her my own.

When you go to a woman for strength to get your deepest questions answered, she becomes an idol. You depend on her. If she's not there, you are lost. And at this moment I felt more lost than I had ever felt in my life.

Going to a woman for strength results in a strange combination of possessiveness and distance. You become possessive because you need her validation of yourself as a man. You depend on her affection.

It also creates distance. In my life, this showed up as passivity. Since I depended on her for affection, I shied away from rocking the boat. Engaging her in a way that might create conflict was simply not an option. So even when I should have stepped in, I didn't. That made her feel very distant.

In other men, distance is created by anger. Because they depend on their wives to answer their questions of love and respect, they end up angry when those questions aren't answered.

In reality, most men are a mix of passivity and anger. Put another way, if we idolize something other than God, we eventually despise and resent it because it ultimately lets us down.

The source of possessiveness and distance goes back to looking to her for life. Anything that I look at to bring me life is an idol. Could it be that I had turned my wife into an idol?

"Are you ready to give her to God?"

I swallowed hard. Something in me knew this wouldn't be easy. "Yes," I answered. I closed my eyes and began to pray:

Jesus, I give her to you. She is your daughter. You made her. You love her more perfectly than I do. You long for her healing and restoration with more intensity and purer motives than I do.

I release all the claims and expectations that I have of her. I release her of the responsibility to comfort me or make me happy. You are my comforter and joy. I release her of all expectation I have for her to validate me as a man. My validation comes from you as my Father.

Jesus, help me fight for her and bring my strength to her out of pure motives. Help me to be concerned for her healing, not for how her healing will affect me.

Jesus, help me release the illusion of control in my life. Teach me to read the wind, discern its direction, and set my sails accordingly.

While I prayed, the weight began to lift. I saw clearly how I had idolized her.

Should you receive love from your wife? Of course; but the first source of

love needs to be from God the Father. "Love The Lord your God with all your heart, soul, mind, and strength" (Mark 12:30). When we do this, the love that we get from our wife overflows naturally, rather than something we try to pull out of them. It's wonderful. When I put my spouse as the primary source of love, I become (co)dependent on her. I'm essentially addicted. If her love is not there, then I am lost.

Am I loved? Do I have what it takes? These questions need to be brought to God. His answer is always a resounding "Yes!"

The next morning, I attended my best friend's church. I was emotionally drained, and worshipping God felt so good. What happened next shocked me.

The worship team started playing a song I'd recently heard called "Stay Amazed":

O Holy God, I stay amazed
You are so much more than words could ever say

O Holy God, I pour out my praise
On the One who never ceases to amaze.

I heard the voice of God speaking in my heart: "Would you be willing to take all of the love that you have for your wife and give it to me?"

"What? That's a lot of love." The song continued:

You are loving beyond measure

Your presence is the treasure I am seeking

You are the all-consuming fire

I am Your desire and You are mine.

Again, I heard the question, but this time it was more like an invitation. "Would you be willing to take all of the love that you have for your wife and give it to me?"

Why did this feel so hard to do? Why did this almost feel like it was wrong?

The chorus started,

I'm pouring out my praise on You. I'm pouring out my love on You.

I did it. Out loud in the middle of the noise of the band, I said, "God, I give all of the love that I have for her to you right now."

At that moment, I felt the embrace of the Father. I'd never felt anything like that before in my life. It was like God was standing behind me with his arms wrapped around me.

The source of your love needs to be the Father. He needs to be the one answering your questions. It was supposed to be like this all along. If you continue to look to your wife for love and validation, you will be devastated.

How do you start? It begins with surrendering your wife to God. Feel free to use the prayer from earlier in this chapter, or use your own words. Put her in the hands of God.

I found that it was helpful to invoke this prayer, releasing her to God every morning during the time that I was fighting for my marriage. It also became useful in times where I was desperate to get her back.

You Need a New Source of Love

It's time to start looking to God as your primary source of love. This has been important all along. This may be the most important thing you can learn during this season.

Looking to God as your primary source of love is tremendously hard. Everything in you craves the love of your wife. However, her love is either gone or, at best, unstable. You need the consistent love of the Father.

If you don't seek love from God along with the answers to your core questions, then you will be drawn to seek love in other places. You'll go to other women to find it, pulling you into relationships that will do further damage to your heart. You'll try to drown out the pain with alcohol or other addictive substances. The best and only answer right now is to seek the love and validation of Father God.

How do you experience the love of the Father? Ask him. Here's how the prayer might start:

Father, my heart is so broken right now. I'm in pain. I desperately need your love. I'm not even sure what that means, but I want to look to you as my primary source of love. I want you to fill me so that I can bring love to my wife rather than depending on her to receive love.

This doesn't happen just once. You have a lot of unmet needs for love, so you'll need to do this repeatedly. When you're overwhelmed, take that as a cue to go back to the Father and ask him for his love.

Spend time with the Father. Pour your heart out to him while you drive or walk. For me, writing down my prayers has been very helpful. Put on some worship music.

The Father wants to answer your biggest questions. Ask him if you are loved. Ask him if you have what it takes. I have a pretty good idea what the answers will be, but you need to hear them for yourself.

Loneliness and Sadness

Sleep can be hard to come by when your life has been turned upside down. One night, I awoke at about 3:00 a.m. The blackness of the night amplified the silence of being alone. After

16 years of sleeping next to my wife, the loneliness of sleeping by myself felt like it might swallow me.

Months earlier, I took for granted that she would always be by my side. Something as simple as her resting next to me would have gone unnoticed. I might have even been annoyed at her snoring, but now I would have given anything to have her beside me, listening to her breathe and feeling her presence.

The ache of loneliness creates a unique kind of pain. In that moment, I couldn't cry. All I could do was lay there, staring into the blackness. I'd never felt this alone, empty, and lost in my life.

About the time I thought the darkness would swallow me, I called out to God.

"Father, are you there?"

Instantly, I felt His presence. I knew in the core of my being that I was not alone. He was with me. There would be many times in the days to come that I would feel lonely, but I was always able to look back to this experience and remember that I wasn't alone.

What Do You Do with Loneliness?

Loneliness can feel like punishment. The worst criminals are sentenced to solitary confinement. Isolation can drive a man mad. What do you do with loneliness?

Realize first that you are not actually alone. The scriptures talk about God's abiding presence. David knew this when he wrote, "Even though I walk through the valley of the shadow of death, I will fear no evil, for you are with me" (Psalm 23:4).

One of the gifts of this season is learning that you are not alone. God is with you at all times.

The Trap of Loneliness

Loneliness can drive you to dangerous places. You long for companionship. Desperation rarely leads us to make life-giving choices. In reality, it was probably desperation to fill a void in her heart that led your wife to adultery. You don't want to be in the same place.

Loneliness can lead you to seek the companionship of a woman who is also lonely. As we discussed earlier, you would be going to her to get strength, not to give it. Two wounded egos seeking solace is not a recipe for a healthy relationship. That can only be found in God.

When you are lonely, you usually don't have great judgement. You risk entangling yourself in an unhealthy relationship. If you are still married, you'll dishonor your vows in the same way your wife did.

Loneliness can drive you online. A recent survey uncovered the top reason men turn to the dark world of Internet sex: loneliness. The world of pornography offers pseudo-companionship that will destroy your heart. After the brief rush of satisfaction, your loneliness will return, compounded with shame. You'll go back for another hit; eventually, you become addicted.

Loneliness can drive you to fantasize about your next relationship. Online dating websites seem innocent, promising a dream for the future. This can be misleading. This is a time where you need to be fighting for your marriage. If your marriage is over, then you need to pursue healing before you offer your heart to another woman.

What to Do with Loneliness

What do you do with loneliness? Know that it is temporary; you won't be here forever. You may find yourself back in your current marriage someday. Maybe you'll get divorced and meet an amazing woman.

Part of this season involves learning to embrace aloneness. It's not a bad thing to learn that you can be okay on your own. This season can be a time where you build a new sense of identity as an individual.

What can you do? Get busy. Maybe there's a project around the house you've been putting off, or a hobby you'd like to rekindle. You've got time. Get off the couch and do something.

Surround yourself with people. This can be hard. I found that I really didn't want to be around people. Being around my married friends made me sad, and they typically didn't have time since they were busy with their families. Find ways to be around people even if it feels uncomfortable.

Another productive way to handle your loneliness is to write down a clear vision of your future. This way, if your marriage is restored, you'll know your goals. If it is not restored, you'll know what kind of woman you want to be with.

When I did this exercise, I wrote down five things:

- Is deeply in love with God
- Has a good relationship with her father
- Positive outlook on life

- Confident
- Is comfortable in her own skin

This exercise allowed me to develop hope in the future. When I did meet the woman who would become my next wife, she fit every one of these items.

The most important thing you can do with loneliness is let it draw you to God. There is a fellowship with the Father, the Son, and the Holy Spirit that can be discovered in this place of loneliness, desperation, and shattered dreams.

The Bible says that God is near to the brokenhearted (see Psalm 34:18). Could it be that God is closer to you now than he has ever been before?

There are places in life that you don't discover until you hit the bottom. Now that she is gone, you're left in a place of loneliness.

How do you find this place with God? Simply ask. "Father, you know where I am. You know my story, and right now, you know the loneliness in my heart. I need you to come for me right now. Be a friend to me. Meet me in my loneliness."

3: Sadness

During the summer following the separation, she thought it would be good for our son if we got together as a family once or twice a week. Everything inside me looked forward to these moments. I wanted so badly for our family and my life to return to normal. Simple things I had taken for granted like sharing a meal together or sitting down to watch a TV show were now gone.

One afternoon, my wife thought it would be good to go to the swimming pool together at the country club with our son. A counseling session earlier that day cut deep into my heart. During the session, my wife revealed that she no longer had any feelings of love for me. Instead, she was struggling with feelings of love for the man that I would later learn she was spending every waking moment with during our separation. All of this happened while she was supposedly "finding out who she was and working on our marriage."

Sitting by the pool, I looked over the top of the magazine I was holding, watching my wife and young son splashing in the water. Everything seemed so perfect and yet so wrong. Everything I valued the most was there in front of me splashing in the pool, and it was slipping away.

I couldn't take it anymore.

My family was being ripped apart. On top of that, my business was struggling to stay alive and the financial noose was beginning to tighten as I'd lost her income.

Tears began streaming down my face. I tried to hide behind the magazine. Clumsily, I excused myself and walked quickly to the car.

When I sat down in the car, everything broke loose. I could barely see to drive home through the tears. I stumbled into the house, landing in what was once our bed, tears now turning to deep sobs of pain. Huddling under the covers, face buried in the pillow, I felt a new level of despair.

The enemy jumped on the situation. For the first time in my life, I contemplated suicide. The voice of the enemy whispered, "It's all over. Everything you have built has crumbled."

A while later, my wife and son returned from the pool. As much as I wanted to pull it together, I couldn't stop crying. Realizing I was hysterical, she escorted my son back out of the house and called two of my best friends to come and intervene.

I could tell they had started praying. The despair started to lift and the enemy backed off. Out of pure exhaustion, I stopped crying.

A few minutes later, my friends stood in the kitchen, not quite sure what to do. Their presence was awkward and consoling. I didn't want to see anybody, but I desperately needed them there. Gradually, the thoughts of ending my life disappeared.

Suicidal Thoughts

Most men experience thoughts of suicide as they watch their marriage and family disintegrate. You are not alone in this.

For some, it's not so much that they want to kill themselves, but that they just want to die. They want the pain and despair to end. For others, it's a bona fide desire to take one's own life. In both cases, the root is the same: the enemy is lying and saying that all hope is lost. Don't believe it.

In this place of hopelessness, however, it feels impossible to see a bright future. Know that there is hope. Recently, as I was working in the yard, I was thinking about how wonderful my life is now. Eight years since the dark days, I now have a beautiful wife who loves me, a happy 14-year-old son, and grand babies from my stepdaughters. I experience more happiness than ever before. I'm so thankful I didn't give in to thoughts of suicide that afternoon.

When you experience thoughts of suicide, or a sense that you just want to die, please call out for help. You are not alone. Call your friends, a pastor, or a mentor. Pray. Force yourself to go outside. Your children need you. The world needs you. Life will get better.

Embracing Grief

This crisis brought new levels of sadness I didn't even know existed. Other than at funerals, I don't think I had cried since I turned ten years old. Now, I was facing uncontrollable tears.

Sadness is the appropriate response. You are losing someone special. Your marriage is dying. It's not much different than a death. Therefore, it would be unnatural not to grieve.

In the months before my wife moved out, one of my older friends had lost his wife to cancer. As we sat on his back porch one evening, he told me that what I was about to go through was going to be harder than dealing with death. I think he was right. While his wife didn't choose to die, mine chose to walk away. He had the finality of a funeral and would never see her again. I would see her all the time, especially in the years until our son became an adult.

The death of a marriage is like losing your best friend and then being haunted by their ghost. If your marriage does end in divorce, chances are you'll see your former wife many times in the years to come.

Dealing with Sadness

What do you do with this deep sadness? How do you handle a flood of unfamiliar emotions and tears?

1. Don't run from sadness

Give yourself permission to be sad. The wise writer of Ecclesiastes said there is a time for everything. There is a time for joy and a time for pain. Right now, this is a time for pain. Something that you valued early is dying. You have little control over it. This is profoundly sad.

For years, you may have pretended that things were fine even when they weren't. There is no longer a need to pretend. It's okay to cry.

I spent most of my life avoiding sadness and pain. In counseling, I learned that when I shut off my heart to emotions like sadness, I also close it to happiness and joy.

As an adult, I became numb. Part of the benefit of this sadness was that dead parts of my heart were beginning to come alive. Even though it was painful, I'd discover later that I had a new capacity for love and joy that I never thought was possible.

Think about surgery. You agree to an operation because the pain has become intolerable. The procedure is painful, but it is only the beginning. After the operation, you go through a period where you experience even more pain than before the surgery. You endure this pain because you know it is part of the healing process.

In the same way, sadness is part of the healing process. You don't have to stay sad forever, but you do need to walk through this valley. Enter into your sadness. It is healthy to let your heart come alive, even if it is through pain.

2. Understand why the pain seems out of proportion

If you've spent most of your life avoiding pain, then sadness feels very unfamiliar. Even worse, if you've spent your life avoiding sadness, you probably have a lot of sad things in your life that you have not yet grieved.

There is a good chance that this will be compounded by sadness for other things you have buried. Maybe you never fully processed your parent's divorce. Friends and family who have gone before you may not have been grieved. Possibly, there have been estranged relationships with parents or friends.

If you find yourself crying tears that seem out of proportion, much of this is due to the fact that you have other "un-grieved" sadness stacked in your heart.

This may be hard to see, but the tears you are crying are healthy because you've needed to cry for a long time. If you hold them back, though, you run the risk of shutting down the part of your heart that you use to love and feel joy. So, as you shed these tears, you are actually opening up new possibilities to love. If your marriage is restored, you can come back as a better man. If it ends and you find a new relationship someday, you'll have much more capacity to love.

3. Let Jesus be present with you in your sadness

Invite Jesus into your sadness. In my times of deepest despair, I cried out words like, "Jesus, please come for me now. I don't know how to handle this." Or, "Jesus, please be with me in my sadness."

David was a man who experienced deep sadness. Here's what he discovered: "The Lord is close to the brokenhearted and saves those who are crushed in spirit" (Psalm 34:18).

No formulas exist for this; you just invite God in. God is near you in your pain. Next time your heart is overwhelmed with sadness, call on him.

4: Denial

The day after I discovered my wife's affair, I spent the night in my good friend's guest bedroom. I was emotionally, mentally, and physically exhausted as the apple cart of my life had just been turned over.

Looking for some perspective the following morning, I headed to a local lake for a walk. Stumbling around the trail, I was desperately trying to make sense of what had happened and what was about to potentially unfold. At the same time, a growing swell of emotions washed over me, feeling at times like they would pull me under as I drowned in a swirl of grief and anger.

Picturing my wife in the arms of another man was too much to process. The implications were overwhelming, so I chose denial of reality because I couldn't handle the pain.

Like most women in this situation, my wife had lied about what was truly happening. There were many versions of the story. At the time, she insisted on separating so she could "work on herself outside of the pressure of the marriage." I believed her.

So, we separated. In that time, I began to work hard on myself. I read books to improve my emotional availability. I hired a counselor to help me fix my issues. I remember the moment when my counselor leaned forward and handed me a book entitled, *I Told Me So.*[3] The book is about how good people deceive themselves and live in denial.

Not wanting to accept the truth, I convinced myself that my wife was doing the same thing. Alone in her executive apartment with the space I had given her, she must be working on herself, seeking forgiveness, and trying to become a better person for our future marriage. I fantasized that she was agonizing over her life, writing in her journal, and reading books about how to get her life back together.

Well, I think you know the reality. My friends certainly did. Her time "alone" was anything but self-reflective. Instead, it was an emotionally charged, alcohol-fueled affair with another man.

While I was somewhat naive to what she was doing, there was a part of me that couldn't deal with the real implications of the truth. So, I chose to live in a state of denial.

Denial is sometimes necessary during a painful event. When you experience physical trauma, such as a broken leg, for example, the body goes into a state of self-protection, sometimes shutting down the pain receptors. The body does this because it knows that the pain would otherwise be too much. Often, patients don't feel the pain until they are stabilized. Then, through the recovery process, pain becomes a familiar friend.

Emotional trauma is the same way. The immediate trauma from discovering your wife is cheating is too much for any man to handle at first. That's understandable. However, at some point, you will feel the pain. During the healing process, it will hurt. This is the point where you need to pay attention.

Denial can become a coping mechanism to avoid pain, just as OxyContin can become a way to dull the pain of a broken leg. Neither of these are long-term solutions. The prescription drug user who becomes addicted to pain pills risks destroying their life, so does the man who stays in the state of denial.

When I talk to men whose wives have cheated, you'd think they would be angry. Certainly, that's a valid emotion we'll address. However, I've discovered that many times, these men are compassionate toward their wives. This is especially true for Christ followers. "She's a really good person," they often say. "She's gotten off track, but she's really working on herself. I'm praying for her and I believe that all things will work together for good."

Some men will say that their wife was deceived or seduced by another man. "She was at a vulnerable point in her life and it's really his fault." While he may be manipulative, it takes two to tango. She has entered this with her eyes wide open. She chose to break her vows. This is as much her fault as it is the other man's.

Others will say with a level of understanding that "she is wounded as a person and God will bring her back." I think this is true, but there are many ways she could respond to her wounded heart. Right now, she has willfully chosen to leave you, giving herself to another man.

I do believe that God will work all things together for the good of those who love him and who have been called according to his purposes.[4] I also believe that can happen in your life. However, you first need to come to honestly assess the situation.

Regardless of how wonderful a person your wife might be, she has had an affair. This means she has given her heart and her body to someone else. They have shared meals together, laughed together, and enjoyed some great sex.

If she's like most women, she feels tremendously guilty, yet she keeps going back to him. All of this is fueled by powerful hormones that accompany any new love. In addition, there is an enemy, the devil, who is cheering all of this on with his lies.

Is there hope? Yes. Can your marriage and trust be restored? Possibly.

Right now, though, it is bad. She is making choices that are profoundly affecting the lives of you and your children. The sooner you acknowledge this, the sooner you can begin to heal and fight for yourself, your kids, and your marriage.

Denial is not your friend; God is. As you begin to accept the reality of what has happened, invite him into it. He will help you. He will walk with you through this valley.

5: Anger and Confusion

As a man who chose to be a peacemaker and avoid conflict before my wife's affair, I didn't have much direct experience with expressing anger. Nor did I anticipate the immediate aftermath: confusion. That changed in this season.

One morning, several weeks after she moved out, I woke up early, alone in the bed we had shared, the first light of the sun peeking around the edges of the curtains. The previous night had been rough, full of restless sleep and dark dreams.

Dealing with Anger

Lying alone in the middle of the bed, I felt surges of anger welling up inside me. Each wave seemed bigger than the last. Like waves on a beach, I'd ride out with deep breaths and hope the next one would be smaller.

For most of my life I'd learned to suppress anger. My father would blow his top when I was young, so I'd made a decision not to explode in response. Like many children, I became a master of suppression, adapting to my environment.

Neurologists call this a "limbic lie." In other words, the limbic system in our brain is the seat of our emotions. It's our fight or flight center—where instinct takes over, even before our higher thinking (i.e., our frontal cortex) kicks in and helps us make a more reasonable decision.

When I was little, my limbic brain, which is all about survival, received the (false) message: "It's safer to pretend you are not upset, rather than to express your emotions." This is because from the time I was a baby, I'd grown up in an environment where yelling was common. My brain had simply adapted to cope and survive. Was it understandable, since my Dad was often "unsafe" when he yelled? Yes. Was it healthy, particularly when I grew older and held onto this limbic lie? No.

I did not learn this truth about my limbic wounds until after my wife had left and I started unpacking my anger with my counselor.

On this particular morning, the waves of anger kept growing. The rage surged to a point where I felt scared of what I was capable of doing. I'd suppressed it for so long that it was like a dormant volcano about to erupt.

In the middle of my rage, I headed to the garage. Picking up a short 2 x 4 piece of wood, I began to act like a mad man, yelling and screaming while slamming the board down onto my workbench and table saw. Finally, exhausted, I collapsed into a heap of tears on the cold concrete floor.

Nothing raises a man's anger more than someone coming after his family. What man wouldn't take a bullet for his wife or children? Nobody was holding me hostage with a gun, but another man had invaded my home. Even worse, my wife had chosen to side with the invader!

Anger is understandable. However, you must point it in the right direction, otherwise you could do great damage to your future. Think about it. How can you fight for your children from a jail cell or with a restraining order?

Ask anyone who has worked in a jail or prison, and they will tell you that the majority of people who commit violent crimes did so in the spur of the moment—as an instant action where their mid-brain (or limbic) instincts took over, rather than their higher thinking and reasoning skills. All it takes is a few moments for you to react to whatever "limbic lie" you are carrying around, and irrevocable damage can take place.

If you want to navigate this season successfully, you must deal with your anger. Find a therapist who understands the root causes of anger. Also, check out Dr. Caroline Leaf, who has written several books on defeating toxic thoughts, including the limbic lies that attach themselves to us when we are very young.

Do Not Make Threats

I knew the man who was having an affair with my wife. Everything in me wanted to threaten this home wrecker. I also knew my tough ex-military friends would have my back. In fact, some of my friends were encouraging me to confront him.

Anger can lead you to make threats. Do not do this. Later on, these threats can come back to haunt you. For example, they could affect your ability to get custody of your children. If the situation calls for a face-to-face or phone conversation, have a third-party present. This will help you avoid a dispute of the facts later on.

You may be a peacemaker like me, or you may have a short-fused temper. Either way, this season will include anger. First, you'll be angry at your wife. Next, you'll be angry at the man (or men) who have pursued her. You may also find yourself angry at God.

Leave Room for God's Wrath

You have been severely wronged. The God of Justice knows this and is aware of every detail regarding your situation. He also hates lying and infidelity.

The Apostle Paul says, "Do not take revenge, my dear friends, but leave room for God's wrath, for it is written: 'It is mine to avenge; I will repay,' says the Lord."[5]

If you take vengeance into your own hands, you don't leave room for God to do his work. God is uncompromising about this. The top ten commandments include adultery on the same list as murder.

"So it is with the man who sleeps with another man's wife. He who embraces her will not go unpunished."[6] The writer of Proverbs assures us that the man sleeping with your wife will be punished.

Paul gets even more serious as he talks to one of his churches that apparently had issues with sexual immorality and infidelity:

It is God's will that you should be sanctified: that you should avoid sexual immorality; that each of you should learn to control your own body in a way that is holy and honorable, not in passionate lust like the pagans, who do not know God; and that in this matter no one should wrong or take advantage of a brother or sister. The Lord will punish all those who commit such sins, as we told you and warned you before.[7]

Of course, you are angry, but if you take your anger and turn it into vengeance, you crowd out the opportunity for God to do his work.

Focus Your Anger

Shortly after I discovered my wife was sleeping with another man, Jim showed up in my living room to give me counsel.

"You know the real target here, right?"

"What are you talking about?" I said.

"The real target is your son."

The enemy's goal is to destroy your family. His primary target is your children.

Therefore, you need to focus on fighting for your children. Pray for them. Spend time with them. Be strong and sensitive to their needs. It's going to be hard because you have no idea where those emotional reserves are going to come from, but it's possible. (More on this later in the book.)

Exercise

Anger is energy. You need to release this energy or it will consume you.

Exercise is mandatory for this season of your life. Ideally, this is the time to sign up to play hockey, rugby, or a similar sport where you get to bang into people! If you can't play a contact sport, then run, mountain bike, or push some weights. Play racquetball with your friends.

Intense exercise helps you metabolize anger. It also gives you the energy you need and helps with the sleep that can be so hard to come by.

Pray

If you haven't prayed before, now is the time to learn. I don't mean just "list prayers", but have a conversation—tell God how ticked off you are. He's heard it all before, and won't be shocked or fall off his throne.

Take a few moments of the day just to be silent and listen for his voice. You truly do need to "cast your anxiety upon the Lord for he cares for you." (I Peter 5:7)

Dealing with Confusion

Our wedding anniversary date was about six weeks after she moved out. Committed to working on the relationship, I scheduled a date at the nicest restaurant in town. Since she had plans with "friends" that evening, we celebrated our anniversary date over lunch.

She asked me to bring our wedding album with me, which seemed like a ray of hope. In preparation, I walked upstairs to the guest bedroom, and opened a wooden chest where we kept special things to find the wedding album. Opening the leather cover, I flipped through the pages, remembering the young man who 17 years earlier had said the vows to a beautifully dressed girl with a radiant smile.

It seemed strange to mark an anniversary during lunch. Businesspeople have lunch. Anniversaries are celebrated over romantic dinners, long weekends, and extended getaways. Since I was fighting for my marriage, however, I had to take what I could get.

The fact that she had asked for the photo album seemed like a good sign. As we flipped through the pages and remembered the day, as desperately as I tried, I couldn't hold back the fountain of tears. On the other side of the table, I watched her analyze the photos with a disconnected analytical look, almost like someone evaluating a crime scene trying to figure out what happened.

"I wanted to see these photos so I could try to reconnect with that person I was almost 20 years ago," she said. That seemed good, but the cold disconnection in her eyes was completely opposite from the deep love I felt in my heart.

Finally, the long lunch was over. She headed her way to be with friends for the holiday weekend. I headed home, photo album in hand, and walked into the empty house.

With no lights on and sunlight streaming through the slits in the closed blinds, I sat on the couch in silence for what must have been hours. My eyes had run out of tears, but my heart was still squeezed with the sadness of the disconnect.

Sitting across from her at lunch, my heart had never been more committed to the relationship and to making it work. Her heart was completely different. She wanted to reconcile in her mind the difference between the young woman in the white dress marrying a young man, and the middle-aged woman in the tight jeans attracted to someone else. The contrast was extreme.

This contrast caused much confusion. I was so focused on making things right that I missed the reality: she didn't care. She was on to the next thing. The only thing she was committed to was finding a graceful way out of the marriage with the least amount of personal shame and public embarrassment.

As your friend, the best advice I can give you is to recognize and accept what is going on. You want to fight for her and the marriage. Right now, she may not.

I found myself looking for any hope that she wanted to fight for the marriage. When you look for something, you'll find it, but you'll also miss many other things. There were shreds of hope, but I misinterpreted them when I chose not to see all of the other signs that offered anything but hope.

Accept Reality

As best as you can, choose reality. Ask God to help you see what's happening. Even when reality seems like more than you can handle, it is your friend right now.

Your wife has made some very dark choices. She has broken her vows to you. At least some part of her heart is attracted to another man. She is emotionally involved with him because that's how a woman's heart works. Accepting this reality will help begin to clear some confusion.

Understand that She is Lying

People who have affairs by default need to lie. Your wife has lied to you and hidden things in order to pull off the affair. Since women are typically better communicators than men, they are usually better liars.

Much of what she is telling you is not true. At best, it's partial truth. Does this make things less confusing? Not necessarily. However, when you know that the person you're talking to most likely is not telling the truth, it helps you to start to sort out reality.

Talk with Friends

Sometimes, it takes close friends to help you see reality. Seek out your "safe brothers" – guys you know will tell it to you straight. Throughout the days of my wife's affair, I found it helpful to have guys that could be honest with me. Everything in me wanted things to work out. I wanted to believe the best about my wife. I wanted to buy into the things she said about needing space to work on herself. I wanted life to go back to normal. This clouded my judgement. My friends were a good buffer for my unreasonably hopeful assessment of the situation.

Get a Counselor

If you find yourself confused, I highly recommend seeing a counselor. They talk with men and women in your situation every day. A counselor will help you fix your blind spots and see what's really happening. Then, they can help you through the process of coping with reality.

6: Separation

Separation is often a reality when she cheats. However, separation brings up many important issues. In this chapter, we'll discuss some of these to give you a framework to make good decisions during this important time.

While my wife moved out over the Memorial Day weekend, I went out of town. During the weekend, she came and got the belongings she would need during the separation. As I drove back on Monday, the pain of walking into my house with her belongings and some of the furniture removed seemed too much to bear.

I asked my friends to go to my house and pray. They walked through each room of the house and prayed blessings over it. I'm pretty sure they did some clean up along the way as well.

That night when I pulled into the garage, there were already lights on in the house. My friends had left, but they wanted me to feel at home. Walking into the living room, I collapsed into a heap of tears. Even as the waves of grief surged through my body, I could feel a peace in my heart.

Who Moves Out?

In many circumstances, a wife who is having an affair will want some space for herself. If she insists on this, I recommend you insist that she be the one to move out, not you.

A few days after I discovered my wife had cheated with another man, she told me she needed some space. She felt suffocated and thought it would be a good idea for us to separate so she could "find herself." In my state of shock and panic trying to keep my family together, I began to find a temporary place to live. Fortunately, an older mentor caught me and gave some good advice.

"She is the one who is running away from the marriage, so she is the one who needs to leave," he said.

Later that day, I told my wife that I didn't want a separation. If she did, she was welcome to move out.

Sadly, she did find an executive apartment that very week. I later learned that the "freedom and space to find herself" meant spending the nights and weekends when she didn't have our son with her boyfriend, while she continued to lie to me and our counselor.

Staying in the house and giving her the option to leave was smart advice. My son, who was five at the time, didn't see his father abandon him and his mom. Unfortunately, he did witness his mom moving out, but that is on her, not on me. Years from now, as my son reflects on his childhood, he'll no doubt have painful memories. The memories, however, will not be of his dad leaving.

What if She Wants to Stay?

While some women want space to "find themselves," other women want to pretend nothing is wrong. They want to have their cake and eat it too, continuing to be the wife and mom while they pursue their affair.

If you confront your wife about the affair and she does not agree to quit immediately and go to counseling, I recommend that you kick her out. Many men think that if they let her stay, things will change. If they do what she asks and try to be a better man, they'll get her back and preserve their family. Rarely have I seen this work out. Instead, by letting her stay, you're basically saying, "It's okay if you cheat on me." At the same time, she gets a husband that's doubling down to please her and take care of things around the house while she continues to indulge her obsession with another man.

What causes a man to stay in the same house with a wife that he knows has given her body and heart to another man? It could be co-dependence. It could be that his identity is so wrapped up in being seen as a successful, godly married man, that to have her move out would make him look bad. It could be that he thinks it's better for the kids.

As hard as it may be, if she's not willing to end the affair, be accountable to you and her friends, and see a counselor, you probably need to separate. Co-dependence is not a good way to live. If your identity is dependent on being seen as successful, I'm sorry—this is your life now. If you think it's better for the kids, consider the impact of them living in the home with your toxic rage simmering below the surface and her brazen disrespect of you. This is not a healthy family.

Should You Stay in Your Current House?

If you have children, you want to keep their lives as stable as possible. Their mother has made choices that are already profoundly affecting their lives. Unless she repents, seeks counsel, and makes some serious changes, she's heading down a road that will bring a lot of heartache.

Right now, she's self-absorbed in the dopamine-induced haze of a new relationship. At some point, that will come to an end. After all, men who cheat with a married woman will most likely do the same thing again with another woman, leaving her alone. Seeking the next high, she'll turn to other men. Alternately, she now has cheating in her blood, so there's a good chance she'll also cheat on the man who she's with now. Either way, it's not a pretty sight for your kids.

The life of a cheating woman on the prowl is anything but stable. Chances are she'll do her best to put on a good public face to look like she's being a good mother. In the long term, however, her lifestyle will create a pattern of instability for the kids as she moves from one relationship to another.

I was fortunate to be able to keep our house throughout the entire process, giving my son a sense of stability during a major upheaval in his life. Over the next few years, his mom would end up moving to several apartments and houses on her journey through multiple boyfriends and husbands.

When we divorced, I assumed the full mortgage for the home. Financially, the payment made things very tight now that I was living on one income. Arguably, the house had way more space than we needed to live, but this was the price I paid to give my son stability during this trying situation.

I realize that financial constraints may keep this from happening for you. If at some point you need to sell your home to downsize, do your best to keep the kids' rooms as similar as possible.

Later on, when I re-married, due to my new wife's gracious attitude and somewhat restricted by financial constraints, we remained in the same house. I did give her a budget and free rein to redecorate the house to make it our own, but in the process, my son kept his familiar bedroom.

In the coming months, there were many times I walked through the house praying for the presence of God to fill the space. Truly, this is a good idea for all of us and a practice I plan to resume.

"Isn't the house haunted with memories?" several of my friends asked. Since my friends prayed for the house, that hasn't been an issue for me. I think we carry memories in our hearts. If the house triggers a memory, that gives me the opportunity to bring it to Father God for healing.

What About the Ring?

One common question is, "Should I continue to wear my wedding ring?" There are different opinions on this. I think you should wear the ring as long as you are still married.

Just because your wife violated her vows doesn't mean that you are free to violate yours. You got married for better or for worse. Right now, it's for worse.

While still legally married, the ring will be a necessary reminder that you are not yet free from the vows you made before God. At times, it may feel like a painful reminder of what you're going through, but so will not having a ring on your finger. The reality is that this is a painful time no matter how you slice it.

Another reason to keep the ring on is other women. The moment you're seen at work and in the community without your ring, the wrong kind of women will notice. You have enough to deal with. You don't need a desperate, clingy woman dragging you into the same type of adulterous relationship as your wife has chosen. Having the ring on may keep some of them at bay.

How to Be Separated

The time leading up to either a divorce or getting back with your wife can be very muddy. Most people call this period "being separated."

If you get divorced, the rules of dividing property, custody of your children, and child support are plainly outlined in the divorce decree. However, before a divorce, things can get very confused during the separation. In this section, we'll explore some practical aspects of handling issues during this time of uncertainty.

As I talk with men about their separation, many of them discover that they are not really separated. They may live in different places and sleep in separate beds, but at an emotional level, they do everything they can to stay connected. All day long, they text and call their wives hoping the relationship will be restored. Many times, they beg for their wife to come back.

Desperation is not attractive. Plus, your wife already has someone who she thinks in the moment is attractive. When she compares the man who she's fallen for with your clingy self, guess who wins that contest?

Looking back on my story, I'm embarrassed at how desperate I was in trying to win back my wife. I can see now that it was anything but attractive to her, especially in her current state of new love. Add to that the spiritual warfare of the enemy whispering in her ear, and my desperation was actually digging a deep grave for our barely alive marriage.

In the same way that desperation is not attractive, anger and bitterness are not either. You have plenty to be angry about right now. Whether you have outbursts of rage or simply seethe with resentment, she'll be able to tell. Emotionally, it will reinforce her choice to go for another man who she thinks loves and understands her.

Here's an idea: what if instead of being desperate or angry, you showed resolve? If she wants a separation, give her what she wants. Let her know you love her and that you're fighting for her and the family. If appropriate, apologize once for anything you've done wrong to hurt or neglect the marriage, but then leave.

Will you have feelings of resentment? Will you be lonely and want to reach out? Of course. Just resolve not to take these feelings to her during the separation. Instead, discuss them with your safe circle of friends and close family. You can also take these feelings to God in prayer.

Desperation and anger will not save your marriage. You might be surprised that the calm, manly resolve you show will probably do more to help than anything. Once the newness of her fling wears off, she may be repentant and want to come home to a man who is stable, calm, and resolved.

Chances are, part of what caused her dissatisfaction in the marriage in the first place (beyond her own personal issues) was that you were clingy and desperate, or that you were angry and jealous. Bringing either of these qualities to the table right now to "fix" your marriage and win her back will most likely have the opposite effect.

Let's face the hard truth in this separation: she has asked for space to "find herself," which almost always means the liberty to pursue another man. She expects that you will be sad, controlling, and angry. These things only reinforce why she's leaving. Why not give her the exact opposite of what she expects?

Truthfully, this is what God wants you to do: surrender the entire mess to him, particularly when it comes to your spouse's heart. The more you disengage at this time, and ask God to be the mediator, the healthier you will be.

When you do need to contact her about your kids, that's understandable, but many men use this time to start a deep conversation or to vent their anger. Resist the urge to do this. Just communicate about the kids and end the conversation.

To me, the best communication method for separation is texting. To this day, I only talk to my now ex-wife if I absolutely have to. When we do talk, it's only about the kids. Text messages are simple and clear when it comes to communicating details about drop offs, doctor's appointments, and schoolwork. Leave it at that.

If she tries to bait you into a deeper conversation, avoid it. Let her know that if she wants to talk about your relationship, you'd welcome an appointment with a counselor. Otherwise, steer clear.

Money

If finances were tight before the separation, they are about to get tighter. Between you and your wife, you are now maintaining two households.

First, do not make any big financial decisions during this time. This will come back to bite you later on, especially if you get divorced. This is not the time to buy a new four-wheeler or sports car. As much as possible, do not take on debt.

Your wife is making bad decisions right now. She probably already has a second cell phone contract she uses to communicate with her boyfriend. She may have opened up new credit cards and her own bank account. She may be running up balances that you don't even know about. As angry as this may make you, the reality is that you do not have control over her life. The more you try to exert control over her, the more you'll push her away.

The important thing right now is to be the responsible one. Tighten up where you can. I'm not an attorney, but I know that if you get to a divorce court and are the one who drained the checking account or bought a garage full of new toys, it won't go well for you. If you do end up reconciling with your wife, at least you'll only be tackling the debt that she rung up during her craziness.

What About the Children?

After my wife left to "find herself", she wanted plenty of "alone time." We had agreed to share our son during the separation. Overall, this worked fairly well. However, there were many times when she asked to shuffle around dates. Being desperate to win her back, most of the time I accommodated her requests. After all, I wanted to be the good husband and I missed seeing my son.

If I had to do things over again, I would not be so quick to accommodate her requests. The schedule changes she wanted were made to facilitate her quest to relive her twenties as she enjoyed her new romance. My flexibility enabled her to suspend the reality that she was not 22, but actually a mother knocking on the door of 40.

When you separate, I recommend you establish some agreed-upon ground rules for the kids. Whatever they are, write them down and give her a copy. Then, stick with them. I'm not saying you need to be a jerk, but for the most part, when she asks if you would "like to have the kids for a bonus night tonight," say "no" or tell her you have made plans.

Let me assure you, the bonus night is not for you. Becoming the chump who takes on her parental responsibilities while she goes out on the town is creating an artificial reality for her, rather than helping the situation.

Separation Agreements

I suggest that if your wife wants to separate, then you should seek some legal counsel. A good lawyer can help you create a separation agreement. Much like a divorce agreement, this document forces both you and your wife to consider how you will handle important things like property, children, and custody during the separation.

While this may create what feels like an unnecessary expense, the money you spend here could avoid huge expenses down the road. If you do get divorced, the terms of the agreement could help make the divorce case smoother.

Beyond the benefits of a separation agreement, the gravity of walking into an attorney's office (or even the suggestion of it) may snap your wife out of her fantasy world as she realizes that she is moving her family toward dissolution.

Here's what you might say or even write in a letter to her:

I realize that you want a separation. I'm willing to give this to you. This introduces a whole new list of questions into our lives about things like finances and how we share the responsibility of the kids. During this time, I want to make sure we have a clear understanding of how things will work so things like money don't come between us. I think we can both agree that we certainly don't want the kids to be a part of the conflict.

To help with this, I've arranged an appointment with an attorney (or mediator) *who has walked other couples in our situation through the questions they need to answer. I'm inviting you to this meeting so we can both have input. As we separate, my hope is that you will find yourself and find a way back to our marriage. In the meantime, working through a separation agreement will ensure that this period goes as smoothly as possible for us and the kids.*

Additionally, I recommend that at a minimum you explore some kind of written custody agreement.

You may be thinking, "Isn't this a little serious?" The reality is that this is a serious situation. You have both kids and money involved. When she receives this letter, it may shake her back into reality. If not, you're setting the stage for a better separation and, ultimately, a smoother transition out of the marriage.

What if She Says She's Sorry and Wants to Come Back?

Right now, your wife is an emotional basket case. She's got the rush of a new love. She faces the insecurity of potentially getting dumped by the man she's sleeping with. She also carries guilt over everything she is doing to destroy you and the kids.

You're a basket case as well. You desperately want to keep your family together. You're lonely, angry at the betrayal, and furious with the home wrecker sleeping with your wife.

It's likely at some point that she may feel sad and apologize. You'll be desperate for love, so you will want to welcome her back home.

The question you have to ask yourself before you welcome her back immediately with open arms is this: "Has anything changed?"

Has she truly changed? Has there been genuine repentance for what she's done? Is she willing to seek counseling or heal the wounds that she's inflicted on herself? Or, did she get dumped by the man she was sleeping with and now wants to come home?

What about you? You've been emotionally steamrolled, taken some deep wounds, and you're exhausted. Trust is the foundation of any relationship. Guess what—there isn't any trust now. She's destroyed it.

The most likely reality is that nothing has changed with her. She may be sorry, but is she repentant? This religiously charged word "repentance" is actually very simple. It means to turn and walk in another direction.

If you truly want to restore your relationship, don't invite her back in right away. Give her the time to prove she is willing to repent. This means a period where she proves her fidelity. Let her demonstrate that she will be faithful to her commitment to cut off all ties with the other man. Let her show that she is willing to follow through on her promise to go to counseling.

At the right time, you can come back together. Until then, I recommend you start this period of reengagement by meeting with a counselor. Just like you made a separation agreement, you can make a reengagement agreement. Similar to the separation agreement, a written reengagement agreement could outline the things you both commit to do as you work toward restoration.

When you're ready, you can renew your vows. However, come back together the right way. Renew your vows before you invite her back into your house and into your bed. Do this only after she has demonstrated the willingness to change and the seeds of trust are starting to bloom.

Reengaging is going to take a lot of counsel, trust, and grace. If you haven't properly prepared for this time, it will be tough to survive.

This may seem extreme to you. After all, aren't you still married? Don't we want to get the family back together for the kids? Yes. However, the stakes are high. What if your wife returns, but hasn't changed? What if six months or a year from now she's back with the same guy or having sex with some other man? How will this affect you and the kids?

Considering the gravity of what was done, the importance of your children, and that without significant changes the odds are this may happen again, I recommend that you reengage with your wife slowly and cautiously.

That means also taking it slow when it comes to sex. Talk to a therapist; some will recommend a period of abstinence at first. Every marriage and situation is different, of course.

You might say or write something like this:

Baby, I love you. I'm so thankful that you want to come back to our marriage. I'm willing to do this. Since I take our relationship and our family so seriously, it's important for me that we reengage with each other in a way that rebuilds trust and sets the foundation for an even better marriage than we had before. Getting there will require some work.

My heart has been deeply wounded and I've already been seeking counsel and asking God to heal me. Your heart has been wounded as well. I know there is some work to be done and I'm willing to give you the space to find healing and to disconnect from the previous relationship. When we're both comfortable, we can begin to reengage in our relationship by meeting with a counselor. I plan on dating you just like we did years ago. At the right time, we can renew our vows to let our kids and close friends know that we're committed to loving each other for the rest of our lives.

If she agrees to a reengagement agreement (as outlined in the sample letter above), you have a good shot at getting your marriage back. If she doesn't agree, at least you know where you stand. As sad as this may be right now, I promise it won't be as sad for you or your kids if she comes back prematurely and then leaves again.

Unless she is repentant, cuts off all contact with her lover, and seeks counsel, separation is usually the right answer. While separated, rather than obsess over her, I recommend that you focus on healing your heart. This is what we will pursue together in the next section.

Phase Two: Recovering Your Heart

Your heart took a huge hit when your wife cheated, so did your masculinity. You can recover your heart and reclaim the parts of your masculinity that were assaulted.

While conventional wisdom says that a blow like this will destroy a man, your wife's affair does not have to leave you incapacitated. Quite the opposite. This has the potential to make you a better man; more confident and whole-hearted than you've ever been before. In this section, you'll discover advice and encouragement to recover your heart.

First, let's set this up with some key observations about our masculine hearts. As men, we have two basic questions and one need.

The two questions every man has are: Am I loved? Do I have what it takes? The basic need of every man is respect.

Before we begin, however, I want to clarify what I mean by masculine heart. I'm not talking about how the world defines masculinity: power, wealth, virility, looks, and achievements. I'm talking about the core of true masculinity—the kind Jesus modeled. Your heart is the core of who you are. A masculine heart has strength, confidence, and security based in your identity as a son, not in your own power or the world's.

7: Overcoming Pain

I remember that beautiful May morning, several days after the initial shock of discovering my wife's infidelity. Another sleepless night gave way to the rising sun.

My heart was crushed. My mind was spinning. In my despair, I turned to God. I didn't want comfort—I wanted an explanation.

For my entire adult life, I'd done my best to be a good man. I went to church every Sunday, gave tithes from every paycheck, and offerings for special projects. I attended Promise Keepers rallies and participated in marriage retreats.

Most recently, my relationship with God had become even more focused, having heard the voice of the Father at a Wild at Heart men's boot camp. I found myself leading other men. I began praying consistently each day.

Part of the prayer I spoke daily over my life and my family was this: "I summon the angels to destroy the kingdom of darkness throughout my kingdom and domain. Destroy all that is raised up against me and establish Your Kingdom throughout my kingdom and domain."

I was taking spiritual leadership more seriously than I ever had before in my life.

Then, that morning at 7:30, I found myself screaming out to God in my backyard: "Why did you allow this to happen?" My marriage wasn't perfect, but it was good. In the midst of all of it,

I had been faithful; I was hopeful for a better future, and I committed to fighting for it.

Purpose in the Pain

I thought that if I did the right things, I would insulate my life from pain. That was now proving not to be true. In this season, I found myself in the middle of more pain than I ever thought I'd bear.

I don't know your story up to this point. You may have been a self-righteous person like me. You may have been a wild child or an angry man. However, our stories now intersect. We both have shattered dreams.

Whether you were the "good guy" who tried to follow all the rules so that you would be safe, or you were the wild and crazy man living recklessly on the edge, you need to know that God didn't cause all this pain to happen in your life, your wife did. God did allow it, though, and if you let him, he will use it to make you a better man.

What do you do with the pain? Larry Crabb offers some insight and hope in his book, *Shattered Dreams*: "Perhaps we are meant to learn that the richest hope permits the deepest suffering, which releases the strongest power, which then produces the greatest joy."

What if this suffering is the pathway to a strength and joy you have never known? You didn't choose to be cheated on; however, you can choose your response. What if you could see pain as a path to growth?

One of the biggest choices you have is your perspective on the situation. Will you give in to despair and allow the pain to destroy you, sending you down dark roads that will damage you and your children's future? Or, will you look pain in the eye and see it as a way to becoming a better man?

The Path of Pain

The dashboard lights in your car tell you if something needs attention. When the "check engine" light illuminates, you have two options. You can ignore it or you can take it to the shop and deal with the problem. If you don't resolve the problem, it will not go away. Keep ignoring the dashboard light and at some point, you will find yourself broken down on the side of the road. Pain is the dashboard light on your heart. It highlights areas that need to be healed.

Throughout our lives, we all accumulate pain through wounds, many of which are relatively small. Our coping mechanism is usually to suppress the pain. As a result, most men carry massive amounts of ignored pain in their hearts.

Here's the challenge: if you have other areas of unresolved pain in your heart, adding that of your wife's infidelity will likely bring to the surface much of the pain from other times in your life that you have suppressed. This can feel overwhelming.

First, let me say that you will be okay. Emotional pain is real. It hurts, and you feel it as much or more than physical pain. Second, the pain does not have to last forever. You can push through it.

My best friend is a physical therapist. Recently, he received an award as an alumnus of the university he attended. In his acceptance speech, he talked about how he "tortured people" for a living. If you have endured physical therapy, you know there is pain involved in healing.

Right now, you have two choices: numb the pain or work through it. If you choose to numb it, you will not recover your life. You will likely become stuck. When a person breaks their leg, there comes a time when they have to get out of bed and learn to walk again.

Likewise, if you don't get out of bed and into the therapist's room, you will remain imprisoned. I suppose you could spend the rest of your life in bed with a slow drip of pain medicine. At some point, though, that would drive you crazy.

The path of pain is like taking a long hike through the mountains. There are going to be some dark valleys as well as some strenuous climbs that require endurance. Then, there will be some moments at the top of peaks where you experience the powerful combination of accomplishment and clarity: you will see things from the top of the mountain like you never have before.

Did I mention there is no map? There is no compass either. Your pain may lead you into some dark valleys. In all of this, remember the words of David in the 23rd Psalm: "Even though I walk through the valley of the shadow of death, I will fear no evil, for you are with me." Jesus will walk with you through every twist and turn in this journey of healing. This means that you do not have to go through the pain alone; if you let him, Jesus will navigate, set your way points, and deliver you to the destination that is best for you.

It also means that you're walking through this pain with someone who created you and knows every moment of your life, even the intimate details of your collapsing marriage. He also specializes in healing. Take the journey with him. There are no shortcuts here.

A Roadmap

How do you navigate this journey through the valley and make it safely out the other side? Here is some advice.

Don't Go Too Fast

Most men try to rush through this valley. If you do, the pain will not get resolved. If you take your time, you'll have the necessary space for healing.

However, issues like this don't get resolved in weeks or even months. I recommend you set a goal of one year for this process. It sounds like a long time. However, a year will go by quickly. You may need a bit more time or perhaps a little less. Either way, you need to surrender the exact timetable to God.

Imagine if you committed the next year of your life to heal. Chances are, you have many years ahead to live. Don't you want to make this time the best possible for yourself and your family? Whether you end up reunited with your wife or married to another wonderful woman, wouldn't it be much better if you came to that relationship with resolved pain rather than a broken heart?

I've always wondered why second marriages have such a high failure rate. Though statistics vary, the majority of second marriages in the U.S. end in divorce. I suspect that one of the main reasons is that we rush through the valley of pain following a traumatic event like an affair. Rather than being intentional about receiving healing, we choose to distract and medicate ourselves with the love of another woman. We end up bringing our broken heart to her. This is a responsibility no woman can bear and a pressure no woman can endure. Thus, the relationship crumbles.

Look, if your marriage is over, I know you want to get on with the next chapter of your life. If you have a shot at restoration with your wife, I know you want to jump right back in. Be cautious, though, as you have been deeply wounded. You need to invest some time in your healing.

Be Intentional

It has been said that "time heals all wounds." That's simply not true. Jesus heals all wounds, especially those of the heart.

Time *doesn't* heal wounds. In fact, unhealed wounds tend to fester if they are not addressed. You can bury them or try to compensate for them. If the wounds are not dealt with, however, they will rear their ugly heads. Since these are wounds of the heart, they will negatively affect your relationships with those closest to you.

You need to be intentional when it comes to the journey of pain. Unlike a pre-planned road trip where you know every stop, this journey will be a little more spontaneous with twists and turns you didn't expect. In all of it, though, the important thing is to acknowledge that you are on a journey. Your goal is to receive healing for your heart.

The journey through the valley of pain is a hard one. To help you stay the course, it's a good idea to have a destination in mind. Where do you want to go with your life? How do you want to be known as a man, a husband, and a father?

Patients that go through physical therapy need to begin with the end in mind. For someone recovering from a broken leg, the goal might simply be to walk again. It may be bigger, like running a marathon. In the painful sessions of therapy, a patient can keep this goal in sight. The goal makes the pain endurable.

Think the same way when it comes to your heart. It's taken a big blow and healing is needed. It will be a painful process, but the goal is a happy life on the other side of the valley.

The brutal truth, though, is deeper: to truly walk into a healthier, better life, God is going to work with you on wounds that go beyond the pain of your divorce. These include wounds from the past that you dragged into your marriage.

Right now would be a good time to pull out your journal. Write down the date one year from today. Then, list what you'd like your heart to look like on that date. What could your life look like if your heart healed? Then, write down some things that would mean a lot to those closest to you: your wife, your children, and your friends.

While you're in this reflective mode, create another list. What will your life look like if you *don't* intentionally go through the valley of pain? How will this affect those closest to you?

Invite Jesus into Your Pain

Don't try to go through the valley of pain alone. Earlier, we quoted Psalm 23: "Even though I go through the valley of the shadow of death, I know you are with me. Your rod and your staff, they comfort me."

Jesus, the Great Shepherd, will go through the valley with you. He knows the path that you need to take. Shepherds lead sheep with a rod and staff. He can lead you through the valley, making sure you visit all of the places you need to go.

Have you ever spent time around sheep? Sure, they look cute in photos grazing in green pastures, but they are not the sharpest animals in the barn. So, Jesus basically says, "Even though you are obstinate and make dumb choices at times, I love you and will guide you." That's kind of funny, but quite true.

What are the places you will visit on this journey? They are the moments where your heart was wounded: events, situations, and conversations. As we said earlier, these painful episodes won't be confined to the years you and your wife were together.

For example, my Dad was a top-blower—a rager at times. In my quest to regain some control in my life, I became the "good kid" who always strove to keep the apple cart upright and on track. For you, trauma might have come in the form of the death of a parent, abuse suffered at the hands of a relative, or something else life-altering.

Jesus was present for every one of the painful events of your life. He knows exactly what was said and done, and he knows how this affected your heart. As these events surface during your journey through the valley of pain, pause and invite Jesus into them.

I'll never forget the taillights fading as she turned the corner to exit our neighborhood. When she would come pick up our son, I'd stand at the front window of the house, watching my family drive away. Most of these moments brought me to my knees in tears.

Those moments seemed to open up a portal directly into my pain. In these times, I had a choice. I could distract myself with a drink or TV binge-watching, or I could pause, open up my journal, and ask Jesus to heal the pain. These moments of pain may be some of the most favorable times of your life because in that raw place, you can access parts of your heart that are normally closed off. You have the opportunity to receive healing in these places. Of course, it will be painful. You're already in pain, though, so why not take advantage of the opportunity to let Jesus do some healing work?

As you spend time with Jesus, invite him into the scenes of your story that are raw at the moment. Each of these painful periods came with messages to your heart. During these moments of pain and in the aftermath, the enemy was there to put his spin on the situation. The Bible calls Satan "the father of lies." Along with his minions, he's always offering an interpretation of these events, looking for you to agree with him, sealing off parts of your heart, and trapping you in destructive ways of thinking.

The enemy delivers his most effective messages through pain. John Eldredge calls these the "messages of the arrows."[9] Ask Jesus to show you the messages that were delivered to your heart by your wife, an emotionally distant parent, an abusive relative, or something else.

In my heart, I heard, "You are alone and you will always be alone. You are a complete failure as a man."

The important thing to do when you identify the messages from these painful moments is to ask Jesus what he thinks. Unlike the lies embedded in the messages from the enemy, Jesus' perspective will be rich in truth that will heal your heart.

You might say something like: "Jesus, I know you were with me that night as I laid on the floor of the empty closet. What did you think about the situation?" Pause. Allow Jesus to speak truth to your heart.

Here's what I heard: "I never left you. I love you and I've always been with you. This situation is not your fault. I'm going to walk with you through this together. You are not a failure. You are going to be alright."

Words like this from Jesus, full of truth and love, are healing balm to a broken heart. They contain truths that we can hang on to in the midst of a time that seems to be spinning out of control. They contain love that we can soak into our lonely and longing hearts.

You may be reading this and thinking, "Come on, I can't hear from Jesus!" If that's the case, why did Jesus tell his disciples, "My sheep listen to my voice; I know them, and they follow me." (John 10:27)? Jesus speaks. If you're not hearing him, maybe it's because you've made an agreement that you can't hear his voice. What if you chose to break that agreement and simply ask Jesus to speak to you?

When Jesus speaks, it most likely won't be an audible voice. Instead, you'll recognize it in your heart. You'll know it because the words will be healing, like water in the desert.

Break Agreements You Have Made

Pain comes with a message from the enemy, and in moments of pain, we often make agreements with the enemy's interpretation of the situation. Sometimes, without our noticing, Satan deftly pins these messages onto the garments of our mind and heart. For example, in my heart, I agreed with the message that I am a total failure in life.

These agreements can define your future. I certainly do not want the enemy's interpretation of my life to define my future. So, what do you do with an agreement? It's simple: out loud, say, "I break the agreement that I am a total failure." Then, ask Jesus to provide his truth to counter the lie embedded in the agreement.

There will be many painful events that will surface in your heart. When you recall them, don't run away in fear. Instead, invite Jesus into the situation.

Jesus is the Great Physician. He will lead you through the valley, providing healing for each of the events that wounded your heart. He's ready and willing to help. Plus, there is no co-pay! All of this is freely given as a gift from the one who loves you and wants to see you healed.

Keep Moving

In your journey through the valley of pain, don't stay too long in one place. While some men rush through the valley, other men set up camp. If you find yourself reliving the same painful event repeatedly, go back to the previous step: identify the messages, break any agreements, and ask Jesus for his interpretation. Then, move on.

If the pain of the event surfaces again, remind yourself of the healing you received. I recommend that you write all of this in a journal. Record how you felt, the messages, and agreements. Most importantly, write down the truth that you hear from Jesus. That way, you can refer back to it if necessary.

These events will always be painful to recall. Even though it has been ten years since my first wife moved out, I still shed some tears when I remember the events. The important thing is that I no longer think of them every day. The pain does not rule my life. I've received enough healing from Jesus that I can write this book.

As you receive healing, keep moving. Many men enshrine their pain, choosing to let it define them. We all know guys like this: bitter, beaten, even belligerent.

Don't be that guy. Receive healing and move forward.

One Step at a Time

Healing for your heart will happen progressively. There is no magic pill you can take, conference you can attend, or doctor you can see who will take care of this all at once.

When the people of Israel crossed over the Jordan River to enter the promised land, God didn't give them the land all at once. Over time, they took small pieces of land until one day they realized that they now had their own country. Why didn't God give it to them all at once? Because he knew if that happened, there was no way they would have secured the land.

Your healing is similar. Jesus will walk with you through the valley of pain. Over a period of time, he will lead you, stopping at various points to bring healing to specific events.

While the sum total of the pain in your life seems overwhelming, Jesus is smart and strategic. He won't ask you to deal with all of it at once. Since he knows you better than you know yourself, he'll begin by healing the things that are most important.

Some of the places Jesus touches and events he brings you to may not seem to be related to your marriage. He may bring you to places of pain, disappointment, or wounding that happened early in your marriage, long before the affair happened. He may bring you to places in your childhood or events that happened with friends or co-workers. Let him heal all of these wounds.

My late friend and mentor, Mike, coached me to invite Jesus into the garden of my heart. I remember his voice as he said, "Jesus, walk row by row through my heart with me, pulling out the weeds and tilling the soil where you see fit." He wants to do this with you. His agenda is healing and wholeness for your life. He's come to bind up your broken heart and set you free.

Embrace the Opportunity

While this season of pain is terrible to walk through, it can actually be a gift. Every man carries around pain, but most never deal with the hurt from their emotional wounds, so the wounds fester, shaping their personalities and damaging their lives.

You have been dealt a wound that is too big to ignore. As a result, you have been thrust into the journey of pain. If you have the courage to walk through this valley, you have the potential to emerge a much stronger and freer man.

Recently, I learned about a friend who had filed for divorce. She was announcing her engagement to a new man. I don't presume to know the entire story. However, I was sad when I realized that she did not take the invitation to go through the valley of pain and receive healing. She moved straight into a new relationship, taking all of the pain with her. She's smiling in her Facebook pictures, but something tells me that the unresolved pain will come back to haunt her.

I have another friend whose wife cheated. He's stuck in life, spending every day reminiscing about his marriage. It's like the pain has become his identity. He's not really dealing with it. He's sad and angry, but not grieving. Instead of transforming into a better man, he's becoming bitter. You can see the bitterness in his eyes.

Another friend made a conscious decision to walk through the valley of pain following her divorce. She spent an entire year grieving. She stayed open and transparent with her friends, family, and community of faith during this time. We all knew what she was doing and we respected her for it. At the end of a year alone, she emerged a bright, radiant person, ready to step into the next chapter of her life. You can see the smile in her eyes. It's the satisfaction of a person who has journeyed through the valley of pain and came out the other end.

You have an opportunity and a choice right now. Will you run to the next woman? Will you take on the pain as your identity? Or, will you walk with Jesus through the valley of pain and receive healing?

If you're ready to receive healing and fight for your future, keep on reading.

8: The Core Questions of Your Heart as a Man

What is your heart as a man? Look at Valentine's Day cards in early February and you'll see lots of pink and red hearts. Chubby cherubs float through the air with arrows. Sappy cards wax poetically about love and romance. All of this available on a folded piece of cardboard for just $5.99 or more. What a racket!

The heart is more than the fluttery feelings of love. In fact, the heart is much more than any emotion. Your heart is the core of everything you are as a man. It's where you do your deepest thinking. It's where you hold your convictions about what is right and wrong. It's the part of you that houses your motives.

Your heart is uniquely masculine. It really doesn't matter if you drive a fully camouflaged 4 x 4, chew tobacco, and shoot guns, or if you are a fashionista who subscribes to *GQ*, you have the heart of a man.

Masculinity is an elusive and misunderstood thing in today's culture. It's like being a man has become one of two caricatures. On one hand, you find the driven man, trying to make things happen and close the deal. On the other hand, you find the man who's all but given up on life. This includes passive men, like Homer Simpson, who are marked by laziness, boredom, and a hearty appetite.

All are seeking answers to the two core questions of a man's heart: Am I loved? Do I have what it takes? When you understand these two questions, you begin to see what drives a man. You also discover the key to healing. Let's unpack each of these questions.

Am I Loved?

If you ever doubted that love is actually one of our core needs, I'm willing to bet you believe it now. When your wife gives her love to someone else, you quickly realize how much you need love.

Seeking the answer to the question of "Am I loved?" begins early in a boy's life. The first place we receive nurturing is from our mothers. In the earliest of days, even before we are born, we feel the love and comfort of a woman. This continues throughout childhood.

Some men are born into a world with loving mothers who nurture them correctly. Others are raised by mothers who look to take love from their children rather than give it to them. Sadly, some men never experience the love of a mother due to infidelity or death.

What was your experience like with your mother? It's a good question to ask because it begins to shed some light on your earliest source of love.

Maybe you had a great mom who set the bar high. You know what it's like to be loved, cherished, and supported. You expected the same out of your wife, but now you find your heart broken.

Maybe you had a mom who was distant or didn't know how to love. Your earliest days began with a love deficiency. You thought that the woman you married would make up for the lack of love. Now, you find yourself in the exact same place.

Core to the masculine heart is the need for love. Here's the problem: no woman can truly answer the question, "Am I loved?"

Why can't women answer this question? The answer is simple: only masculinity can bestow masculinity. You cannot get masculinity from a woman; you can only give it to her. Masculinity must come through masculine sources: fathers, other men, and ultimately, Father God.

The problem is that virtually every man eventually takes this question of love to women. The first time a teenage boy notices a girl, his heart says, "My mom *had* to love me, but I wonder if this girl will *choose* to love me?"

Few boys make it through their teen and early adult years without getting their hearts broken by at least one girl. Desperately seeking the answer to the question of whether we are loved, we dust ourselves off and go after the next woman.

Someday, we find one we want to marry. We pop the question. She says yes. We buy the ring, rent a tux, and make the vows, all while figuring that we've now taken care of this question. "I'll be loved for the rest of my life," we reason. "After all, it's till death do us part!"

Marriage reveals our hunger to answer the question of lovability. It also quickly reveals that our wife isn't the ultimate source of the answer. Shortly after the honeymoon, we realize that things might not be working the way we thought. She can make us feel great, but she can also cut us off at the knees. We crave her attention.

When we come to her, desperate and needy to feel loved, eventually she'll get resentful. Over the years, the pressure of this resentment builds up. As you continue to demand her to answer the question, "Yes, baby, you are loved," she will feel more pressure and pull back. Your response is to be more demanding. This can become a vicious cycle.

In many ways, marriage becomes a series of unspoken contracts laced with expectation. We figure that if we serve her needs, she'll serve ours. If we provide for the family, take her on some dates, and do the dishes, she'll reciprocate with the love that we crave.

You bust your tail working, sacrifice money and time for the family, and spend weekends doing things around the house. Surely you should be loved in return. After all, "I've done what she wants," you reason, "so I deserve love in return."

However, it doesn't work that way. Your perspective is skewed: love was never meant to be bartered in exchange for service and dedication. Plus, if there is one thing that crushes love, it's the pressure of expectation. Your need to know you are loved squashes out the love that you so desperately want.

So, what you have is the foundation of a marriage where false idols of expectation and performance are being forged in the furnace of false intimacy. Several years into the marriage, the affection dries up. She avoids sex. When she does put out, you can tell that she's just trying to do her duty as a good wife. The answer to the question you hoped for never came. Instead, the answer was, "Nope, I'm not loved."

Where can you get the answer to the core question of your masculine identity, "Am I loved?" The primary source for the answer to this question is Father God. You must know you are loved by God. Then, you can enjoy the love of a woman without demanding it. Instead of going to her to get love, you can actually bring love to her.

Now, in the aftermath of your wife's affair, you find yourself in a big pickle because the answer to the question just became worse: "Not only am I not lovable, she found someone else to love."

Recently, a man shared his story with me about how once he got married, sex became something that happened only every few months. This crushed him. To make matters worse, once they separated, she was quickly in a relationship with another man. The thought of this other man receiving the love that he so deeply craved was overwhelming. Now in his fifties, as he told me his story, I could see the pain still present in his eyes.

Not receiving love from my wife and then watching her give her love to another man may be the most pain I have ever encountered. I went into marriage expecting that I would consistently hear the answer, "Yes, you are loved." When it didn't seem to come, the lie in my heart was that I was going to have to work to be loved. So, I did all the right things: I worked hard; I was involved in a church; I tried to make things special with sweet letters, dates, and vacations. I wasn't a workaholic. I tried to be her Jesus and failed.

Still, the answer to my question was incomplete. She was there. I had a wife. She was faithful and even respectful, but I didn't feel loved. Then, after I found out she was having an affair, any sense of love that I had from her was gone.

I now realize, of course, that she didn't get her Jesus needs met in me. Rather than turning to Christ, though, she simply turned to a new guy. It's logical, if you think about it.

As you reflect on all of this, the temptation is to analyze your experience, your marriage, her life, and why it didn't work. Let's not do that right now. Instead, consider how has the question of "Am I loved" been answered in your life? What have you learned?

When my wife moved out for another man, I was shocked at how much it affected me. Of course, you would expect emotions of sadness, jealousy, and anger, but what I experienced felt different than that. There was a part of me that thought I would die without her.

I realized that there was something more at work here than just being sad about the broken relationship. When I got honest, I understood that I looked to my wife for life. Just as my body requires oxygen, it was as if my heart required her love. Just as I would be gasping for air if I was underwater, I felt my heart gasping for her love.

When you don't first bring your question, "Am I loved?", to God, you give an imperfect substitute the power to bring you life. For me, that was my wife. You also give her the power to take it away. While this sounds romantic, it can become very toxic. If your heart desperately needs love, you'll do anything to get it. This will lead you to approach restoring your marriage with desperation. In the meantime, it may also lead you to pursue other women for the answer.

Where do you get the answer to this question? Jesus' disciple, John, says it well: "We love because he first loved us."[10] We need to hear the answer to this question from our Father God. When we receive love from him, we find that we don't desperately need love from a woman. Instead, we find that we can bring love to her—we have it in excess.

When you receive the answer to your question, "Am I loved?", from God, any love you receive from your wife is a bonus. Since you do not desperately need it, you can enjoy it.

Now that you are faced with the absence of your wife, you can turn to God and ask him, "Am I loved?" As you hear the answer from God, you can feel sad about your marriage, but you won't feel like you are going to die.

Do I Have What it Takes?

The second core question is, "Do I have what it takes?" Can I come through? Am I enough to provide for and protect my family?

As men, we get hard answers to this question throughout life. Work is difficult. We find pressure to perform. Promotions go to someone else. Re-orgs leave us without a job. Just the daily grind in itself is rough. Despite the struggle, there are moments where we come through at work and we get the affirmative answer, "Yes, you have what it takes."

Inside marriage, the answer to "Do I have what it takes?" becomes muddier. Most men get frustrated here on a regular basis. They feel like they have fallen short. Maybe their wife continually reinforces this message. We end up feeling like a failure.

This frustration gets taken to the next level when your wife chooses another man over you. The answer now is a loud and clear "No, you do not have what it takes!"

Failure is the biggest fear of every man. We are afraid we don't have what it takes. We fear that, ultimately, everything will come crashing down.

Just like a man's need for love causes him to become desperate, his fear of failure causes him to control. We become fixers, always trying to control things that seem out of control. That control suffocates a marriage. When a man's wife leaves, that need for control does not go away, it only gets intensified.

When I discovered that my wife was cheating, I dove into fix-it mode. She said that I was emotionally unavailable, so I committed to becoming emotionally available. When I noticed that I wasn't in as good of shape as the man she chose, I hit the gym and bought new clothes.

Sure, there is something good about a willingness to work on yourself. However, I noticed that what was happening in my heart was so much more. It was a striving to be better than the man she had chosen. I wanted to hear a "Yes!" to "Do I have what it takes?"

Really, what we're looking for here is for our wife to validate us as a man. When we come through, we feel great about ourselves. When we don't come through, we try harder. When she leaves for another man, we feel terrible.

The problem is that when you give her the power to *validate* you, she also gets the power to *invalidate* you. When I didn't feel loved by my wife, I felt like I couldn't breathe. When I didn't feel validated by my wife, I felt powerless.

This can lead to depression and hopelessness. Maybe you are there right now. However, you don't have to give her the power to invalidate you as a man; you can find it somewhere else.

Where to Get the Right Answers

The process of recovery begins with taking your two core questions to a different source. As John Eldredge observes, "Only masculinity can bestow masculinity." As men, we need to hear the answers to these questions from our father and other men. Only then are we able to move forward in strength with a full heart.

You need to look to your fathers and brothers. They are the ones who can help you work out these needs for validation. Bring up the word "father" and many men have a very negative reaction. While a few had a great fathering experience, the majority of us had imperfect fathers. Some had absent fathers; some were abusive.

A father is supposed to answer these questions in the heart of a boy, a young man, and even a full-grown man. Out of the wounds they took in life, many of our fathers did not do a good job. Needing answers to our core questions, most of us ended up looking to women for them.

What do you do with this void of fatherlessness now that you are a man? Is it too late? Not at all. In fact, this is the perfect time to receive the answers from fathers.

Look to God

First, you can look to God. When Jesus' disciples ask him to show them how to pray, he uttered two words that shook the foundations of the world and changed everything. As Jesus begins the model prayer, he says, "Our Father."

Until that moment, God's chosen people wouldn't even utter the name of God. When they wrote God's name, they omitted the vowels out of reverence. He was known as the Lord Almighty, Jehovah, YHWH. Every discussion of God revolved around his power and majesty. Then, Jesus came and addressed God in the most familiar and intimate of ways as "Father."

Yes, God is all powerful, holy, and should be worshiped in reverence and awe. However, he is also your father. In Romans, Chapter 8, Paul clarifies this new reality when he says, "Those who are led by the Spirit of God are the sons of God." You have been given a spirit of sonship. God wants to be your father.

As much as you address God in reverence, he also invites you to address him in familiarity. Jesus called God "Abba", which is similar to a loving term like "Papa."

When you embrace God as your Papa, he begins to answer your questions in ways a woman never could. When you feel unloved, you can turn to Papa God and ask him how he feels about you. When you feel like you don't have what it takes as a man, you can ask him for guidance.

Many men tend to see God as a righteous judge, ready to condemn them for every failure, because their earthly father acted as such. As much as God is holy and righteous, though, he is even more loving. His essence is love. That's why he sent his son to die for you. He didn't just want to erase your sins, he also wanted to invite you into his family, literally adopting you as a son.

You might even pause right now and ask God to make this real in your life. You could say something like this: "God, I receive you now as my Father. I receive the spirit of sonship. Help me know deep in my heart that I am loved as a son. I invite you to speak to me. I'm broken right now. I feel like a failure. I need to hear from you that I have what it takes."

You can end with a simple question: "Father, what do you think about me as a man?"

Pay attention to what you hear in your heart and write it down. Hearing these words from Father God can change everything. When you experience this for the first time, you'll want to do it repeatedly. Fortunately, the invitation is an open one. When you feel unloved, alone, and like a failure, reach out to Papa and receive the spirit of sonship.

Look to Older Men

In addition to going to God for answers, I encourage you to seek the counsel and friendship of older men. Before my wife left, I didn't have many older mentors in my life. Those that were in my life were kept at arm's length. I wanted older men to respect me as a man, so I played like I had it all together. The end result was very few close male friends.

After my wife left, I began to build authentic relationships with several older men in my life who became father figures to me. Each of them brought a different perspective to the situation, but they all had one thing in common: they were calm. Life and walking with God had shown them that everything was going to be okay.

Here's something I also learned from older guys who had walked through the fire. It's not like "everything" was going to be okay. A lot of very specific, bad things continued to happen. That's life! However, the biggest things, such as my self-worth, validation, and destiny, were going to be okay. I discovered how to relax in the middle of a crisis.

Look for mature men who you can speak to about your life. I'm not talking about the crusty old men who are full of bitterness for their unfulfilled lives, but rather men who are confident, quiet, and self-assured.

These men have been through the valley of pain at least once in their life. They know how to navigate the darkness and come out the other side. Their stories, advice, and encouragement will be tremendously helpful to you.

In addition to the guidance, these men can answer your questions. Feeling fatherly love from an older man lets you know that you are loved. Hearing a fatherly voice of confidence lets you know that you have what it takes. When these answers come from a seasoned man, you believe them.

Remember that opening scene in Germania at the start of *Gladiator*? General Maximus is at the pinnacle of his military career, yet in the presence of the Emperor Marcus Aurelius, he is like an obedient son. Even though we don't know what happened to Maximus' real father, we don't need to. The older, wiser Marcus Aurelius says to his greatest general, "You are the son that I should have had." This is what we yearn for as men: an older man whom we respect, but who also respects us, flaws and all.

Look to Brothers

You can also look for answers from men who are your age and in the same stage of your life.

Shortly before my wife left, I began developing deep relationships with other men. A group of us had been a part of a weekend event where we had shared intimate details of our stories with each other late one night around a campfire. Following that event, we began to do life together, communicating regularly, and praying for each other.

Until this moment, I didn't really have many friends. The ones I had were mainly surface-level relationships. We rarely talked about matters of the heart. Looking back now, I could see that the main reason I held back in friendships with other men was that I was afraid I didn't have what it takes. Therefore, I felt unable to fit in and be loved by them. What I didn't realize is that it was precisely other men who could answer this question.

This fellowship of brothers was a lifesaver as I fought for my marriage and to rebuild my life. They rallied around me, checking on me when I was down. They prayed for, encouraged, and just sat with me. They showed up on dark days when I wasn't sure if I could even live another day. They validated that I have what it takes to make it through the hard season.

This is the time to look for other men in your life for encouragement. Even if you have been a lone ranger up to this point, don't worry. Lift your head up and look for men who can be father figures and friends. After all, it has been said that when the student is ready, the teacher will appear.

Bringing Strength

Ultimately, you must get answers to your core questions from Father God, older men, and brothers so that you don't have to get them from your wife. Instead of desperately needing to get your strength from her, you can bring her strength. You'll need this strength if you reconcile, if you find yourself single, and if you get married again someday.

However, where does this strength come from? It comes from Jesus, your father figures, and your brothers.

Right now, I encourage you to take your questions to Father God. If you don't have a relationship with God, I can't think of a better and more important time to get started. The Bible says in Romans 10:9 that if you confess with your mouth and believe in your heart that Jesus is the son of God, you will be saved.

You might say something like,

Jesus, I need you. My heart is broken. I confess that I've tried doing life on my own and it hasn't worked. I need your love and to know I have what it takes. I accept your free gift of forgiveness and healing that came from the wounds you took on the cross. I need the power that is available to me through your resurrection from the dead. I need your guidance as I walk through this valley of pain.

Now, ask him to send men into your life to be mentors and brothers. There may be some relationships in your life that you can rekindle. The important thing is to put yourself in a fellowship of men that can love, encourage, and coach you through this season.

Beware of false substitutes. There are men who can point you in the wrong direction. The group of guys at the bar who are distracting themselves from their pain and chasing other women are not the place to find answers. They may be having a good time, but they are stuck in an endless cycle of looking to women for answers, feeling temporarily validated in the conquest, and then being alone. I promise, you don't want this to be your story.

As you get the answers to your core questions "Am I loved?" and "Do I have what it takes?" from other men, your heart will begin to heal. You will begin to recover the strength that you will need to move forward in confidence

9: Recalibrate Your Heart

Years ago, I had an old ski boat. After sitting for a few winters, I didn't realize there was water in the system. When I went to start it up one spring, I discovered that the engine block was cracked. Without that expensive repair, the old boat was useless.

One afternoon, a friend of mine stopped by. Seeing the boat in my driveway, he asked what I was going to do with it. Knowing that it was useless with a cracked engine block, I said that I was going to find a junk yard that would take it. Always wanting a boat of his own, my friend said that he would be happy to take it off my hands. I was happy to get it off my driveway, so I let him have it.

Thinking that he was going to bring it to a junk yard for a small amount of cash, I was surprised several months later when I saw the boat in his driveway. As it turned out, my friend was optimistic about the boat. He began cleaning and refinishing the hull. In the cabin, he replaced the vinyl on several seats and rebuilt part of the console. He even wired in a new stereo system.

The boat looked great. The problem was that he didn't bother to lift the hood, thinking he'd get around to fixing the engine after he cleaned up the boat.

By now, you can probably guess the end of the story. When he brought the boat to a mechanic, the cost to repair or replace the engine was much more than it was worth. He ended up taking the boat to the junk yard, having wasted months of time and money.

Much like my friend who longed to have a boat on the lake, you probably are longing for your life to return to normal.

Here's the problem. Your heart is broken. Similar to the cracked engine block on the boat, until your heart is fixed, it's pointless to work on other things.

You begin with recovering your heart. In this chapter, you will get a template for how to take this journey. We'll explore the shifts that you need to make and how you can pursue healing.

From Desperation to Confidence

The first shift is to move from desperation to confidence. I felt desperate for my life to get back to "normal" and for my marriage to be restored. Much of that had to do with the realities discussed in the previous chapter where I was taking my core questions to my wife. This made me desperate for her love.

Desperation is not attractive and makes you vulnerable. While it may feel like your wife will be moved by your need for her, chances are your desperate need for love and validation helped drive her away in the first place.

After a while, desperation will drive you to other places for love and validation. It's in this moment that many men find themselves vulnerable to having an affair themselves, doing things they swore they'd never do.

Sam's wife of 12 years was having an affair with her boss. Sure, marriage wasn't perfect, but they had a son and a young daughter. Life was busy with each of them working. Most weekends, she served at their church. They were both involved in a small group, regularly hosting events in their home. To him, everything looked like it was going well.

They had met in their junior year of college at a private Christian school. She'd been brought up in church. Even though his family years were rocky, it felt good knowing that he was married to a good girl from a great family.

When he discovered his wife was sleeping with her boss, his world fell apart. It felt like a dagger through his heart. The anger that he thought was under control boiled to the surface. At the same time, sadness washed over his heart as he began to realize the impact this would have on his boys.

After she moved out, he found himself frustrated and alone. During this time, he shared his frustrations with several co-workers. One of them began to really identify with him. It wasn't long before the friendship turned into passionate sexual encounters between two people desperate for love.

Not long into the affair, she moved on, crushing his heart. To make matters worse, this was now a strained dynamic in their small workgroup, leading to complications that almost cost him his job.

Don't be the guy in the story above. The most helpful and honest thing you can do right now is to acknowledge your desperation, rather than to act on it in regrettable ways. Your heart has always been desperate for love. You've just been bringing your questions to the wrong place.

In this season, your confidence has been destroyed. When a woman cheats on a man, he hears, "I am not loved and I don't have what it takes."

What do you do with this desperation and lack of confidence? I recommend you turn toward God. Your desperate need for love is real. Pause for a second: what I just said is really critical. Your need for love is normal, natural, and not something to be ashamed of! God created us to love and be loved. Love is written into your emotional, mental, and spiritual DNA as a human being. We literally die—emotionally and otherwise—if we don't have love.

Acknowledge that you desperately need God's love. Tell him you need to hear you have what it takes.

Ask God to rebuild your confidence as a man. Most of the confidence that men display is really false; it's built on ego and bravado. If you lack confidence right now, it's because it was built on superficial things like job, income, and looks.

After you talk to God about your need for love, "seal" the acknowledgment by telling at least one other trusted male friend or mentor that you are in need of love. It might be a little awkward or hard to admit, but do it.

You can rebuild yourself based upon a genuine confidence resting on the solid foundation of God, which you can carry through the rest of your life. All of this requires spending time with God.

Spending time with God doesn't always mean sitting down with a Bible in front of you. For me, it looked like taking a long walk without headphones, listening to my heart and talking with God. Sometimes, I would head out into the mountains for the day, talking with God on the drive or as I sat on the edge of a cliff. I spent time with God playing worship songs on my guitar, or late at night just sitting on my front porch smoking a great cigar and watching the stars.

These times with God became a lifeline for me. Up until this point in my life, I hadn't really ever spent extended times with God outside of church and a somewhat sporadic daily devotion. In this season of desperation, I discovered that turning my fears and worries to God was the key to my survival. Ultimately, it rebuilt the confidence I needed as a man.

From Striving to Trust

When my wife left, I became obsessed with finding out what went wrong. I dove headfirst into books on relationships, marriage, personality, and anything else I could find. I journaled and wrote letters. Then, I would show up on the doorstep of her apartment, hoping to have long conversations about what I was learning. I wanted to show her that I was working to be a better man. I hoped she would see it and return to me.

Striving is not your friend. To her, it looks pathetic and unattractive. Your striving looks especially desperate in contrast with the fun she's having with her new-found lover.

Striving is exhausting. All day and all night your mind races, trying to figure out how win her back. You can hardly focus on anything else. Not only does this consume your personal time, it also affects your ability to work.

Striving distracts you from taking care of your children. They need you right now. Instead, you're spending every free moment reading books, listening to podcasts, and watching YouTube videos on how to fix your marriage.

All of this reveals that you think the situation is mostly your fault and that if you do things differently, she'll come back.

Suddenly, you've put yourself on the cross instead of Jesus. Does this sound crazy? Well, you are trying to save your marriage by yourself, rather than following God's leading. You need to admit this is not possible without God at the center of things.

To compound the chaos, chances are she's been telling you that this is all your fault. If you had been different, she wouldn't have felt the need to cheat. While some of this may be true, your "seeing the light" and franticly trying to change will not fix the situation.

You need to know that her decision to cheat was about more than your failings as a husband. She chose to violate her vows. While you may not have fulfilled everything she expected from you, the reality is that she was probably looking to you to provide things a man could never really provide. Just as you need to bring your core questions to God, she needs to do the same.

Even as you read this, do you feel the urge to pick up the phone and explain your new-found insights to her? Don't do it! Instead, pause and take a deep breath. There is no magic bullet or perfect insight that is going to fix this. Even if you had the perfect piece of wisdom, chances are she's not in the place to receive it.

What if instead of striving, you choose to trust God? I define trust as "the absence of freaking out." Instead of desperately trying to fix everything, what if you chose to rest in God? In essence, you say something like: "Father God, this is beyond my ability to fix. I trust that you love me. I trust that you love her. I trust that you are for my family. I give it all to you right now because I know that it is in good hands."

As you do this, will God show you some things you can change? Sure, but you can work on these together with him, outside of the pressure of striving.

When you notice that you are striving, pause. Ask God: "Father, am I right?" When he says "yes," ask him what to do. Ask him to bring you rest.

If you do feel compelled to share an insight with your wife, pause. Ask God, "Is this something I should share with her now?" Listen. Maybe the answer is "Yes." Most of the time, the answer will be "No, just hold onto that for now." Remember, she likely is not in the place to receive insight from you. Write it down so that you can share it at the right time.

This battle to rest may be one of the hardest ones you face during this hellish time. Slowing down, staying calm, and focusing your efforts on resting in God is not easy to do at first. However, once you enter into God's presence and *practice* surrendering your situation to him, it will become easier.

Who knows? When your wife sees your calm confidence coming from a place of rest, she may find it attractive. If she doesn't and the marriage ends, I can guarantee you that the next woman that God brings you will be attracted to a man who isn't striving and lives in rest.

From Control to Release

Right now, you probably feel like you have lost control of your life. You certainly can't control your wife's actions. Your kids have been affected, but you can't control how they react to the new realities in their world.

When a man loses control, he typically grasps for anything he can control. For example, you may still have some influence over your wife's finances. To compensate for the other areas in her life you can't run, you might double down on controlling money.

Ask most women who are in affairs on why they left and a common answer will be that they felt controlled. I'm not saying this justifies your wife's actions or that it is even the true reason she left. However, if your wife felt controlled and that was part of what motivated her to leave the relationship, how effective do you think it will be for you to try and control anything right now?

Control is an issue for most men. We want to feel in control of our lives, and it leads us to try to control others. We get rigid in our relationships, and we impose unnecessary rules. We go overboard, obsessed with compliance.

Control looks good on the surface. After all, who doesn't admire someone who leads a disciplined life? The problem is that relationships suffocate in this atmosphere. We were made to live free. The more we try to control others, the more they resist and grow to resent us.

Why do you feel the need for control? Maybe your desire for control comes from fear. You're afraid that it is all going to fall apart, so you do your best to limit risk. This can show up in the way you tightly manage money. Maybe it manifests in the restrictions you put on your kids.

Perhaps your desire for control comes from jealousy. You're concerned that other men might look at your beautiful wife the wrong way, so you try to exert control over how she dresses or whether she goes places on her own.

Maybe your desire for control is driven by insecurity. You don't feel like you have what it takes as a man, so you hold on to what you do have, such as your marriage.

Maybe your desire for control comes from frustration. At your workplace, you report to a dominating boss who has control issues. (How does that feel?) You don't have control over most of your day, so when you get home, you feel like that's the one place you can control.

So, what do you do with the drive to control? First, acknowledge that it is an illusion. What makes you think you can control another human being? Why are you so obsessed with it?

Since giving up control is so hard, I recommend that you let her go. Out loud, you might say something like, "I release Mary. I acknowledge that while I love her, she is her own person and I cannot control her. I put her in the hands of God and I release any and all attempts to control her life."

Control is so deep inside most of us as men that it may take some time to get to the root of it. I recommend you take a deep dive on this. What's driving your need control? Go back through the reasons above and have an honest conversation with yourself. If you're struggling here, engage a counselor to walk you through this.

What do you put in place of control? Trust. I learned to trust that God was ultimately in control of everything. When I felt out of control, I turned toward him. Interestingly, in God's version of control, he doesn't seem to exert very much. He gives all of us the space to love him and the space to fail. Then, when we do fail, he is there to love us.

Releasing control feels risky at first. However, I discovered that it opened up a lot of freedom in my life. I became free to love other people for who they are. This is incredibly attractive. It may help you win back your wife's heart. If not, it will help in a future relationship. It will also help you win your kids' hearts as you love them through this season.

You may be bristling at this advice right now. The desire for control when your life is spinning out of control is powerful. Just remember, control is an illusion. Let go of it and you will find new levels of freedom in your heart. It's this freedom that you will need to move forward.

Here's an "upside down" truth: when you surrender, God takes over; when you give up, he steps up; and when you let go, he takes control.

From Despair to Desire

During this dark time, despair can settle in. You're watching your life crumble around you. The one person you put all of your hope and energy into has left for another man. It feels hopeless.

Despair says that all is lost, things will never return to normal, and life is forever ruined. These are all lies.

Despair is simply the absence of hope. The enemy will batter away at the walls of your heart and soul right now, trying to convince you that there is no hope. Even worse, you may not believe that you can *dare* to hope at this point.

If you invest in hope, that means you have to open yourself up again to potential disappointment. That's one mother of a big fear, right there. Think about that: what sane person wants to get their hopes up after they've been dashed down lower than ever before?

The outward manifestation of hopelessness is despair. It's the lack of hope in action. It will lead to poor choices that will hurt your heart and affect your children. It keeps you stuck and saps any remaining energy from your body.

What do you do with despair? Counteract it with desire. Desire is the outward, visible sign of hope rejuvenated. In order to have the desire to move on, get better, and trust God in this mess, you must utterly surrender of all your circumstances to a father who sees, knows, and understands your wounds.

In Psalm 27, David gives some great advice. He says, "I would have despaired unless I believed I would see the goodness of the Lord in the land of the living."[11]

You will see the goodness of the Lord in your life. The only way these dark days will last forever is if you let them. There will be a valley of pain to travel through, but there is life on the other side and it can be very good.

That happens when the dark, raw ingredients of despair and hopelessness are converted into the high-octane fuel of hope and desire. This is the elixir that will re-start the engine of your heart, and which God will use to transport you to a better place.

The antidote to despair, therefore, is desire. What are your deepest desires for your life when it comes to a relationship with a woman? In this time of sadness, this seems like a frivolous and even cruel question to ask. However, I discovered that pondering the answer was the key to avoiding despair.

Now that you have experience in marriage and some years of living behind you, what would you want your marriage to look like if you could start again?

The reality is that should your marriage be restored, you'll need to make a fresh start. You certainly don't want to walk back into the same situation you had previously. Wise therapists will tell couples recovering from an affair that they can't rebuild their old marriage; instead, they need to start a new one.

If you find yourself divorced and someday dating, you'll also get a fresh start. In either case, it's important to know what you're aiming for.

Exploring your true desires helps you avoid false substitutes. Between pornography and a seemingly endless supply of lonely middle-aged women, there will be many false opportunities to relieve your despair. I discovered that I knew what I really wanted; these substitutes were simply not appealing because I could see them for what they were.

Desire brings hope in the midst of pain. It brings clarity in the midst of confusion. It brings light in a place of darkness.

When you explore your desires, you uncover the core of who you really are as a man. This will call strength out of you that you didn't know you had, and give you something to aim toward and pray for. It will rekindle direction and purpose in your life.

There will likely be tears when you realize how far your life has veered from the direction of your desires. However, these tears will also reveal the deepest longings in your heart. Your core desires are the path to healing. Tears may be embarrassing or feel just...wrong. But think about how long it's been since you cried. For some guys, it's been decades. (For others, it was yesterday.) Tears are powerful, precious pieces of your healing; let them flow.

In my darkest season, I went through the exercise of desire. It was prompted by picking up what has now become one of my favorite books: *Desire* by John Eldredge. He took me on a journey. At the time, it felt reckless and even dangerous to consider my desires. However, I realized that these desires were already in my heart; they were just buried under crushing layers of hurt and disappointment.

When I brought my desires to the surface, I realized that they were the fuel of my despair. The difference between my current situation and my desires caused my discouragement. When I became clear about my desires, it reinvigorated my fight for my marriage. It re-started the sputtering engine of hope in my heart.

Ultimately, my marriage failed. Had it not, I would have walked into the restoration phase of my marriage with a true vision for what I wanted instead of just settling for the status quo, which would have ended up in the same situation of dissatisfaction and infidelity. Knowing what you want will help you down the road if you get a shot at restoring your marriage.

After my marriage ended, I knew exactly what I wanted from a relationship. I was clear about my desires. When the right person came along, I recognized her. As we got to know each other, I shared my goals for life and marriage. She shared hers. When we did get married, we were able to build our life on this foundation.

Many other men I know were not clear about their desires. When their wives left, they went after substitutes. Some doubled down on porn; some even hired prostitutes. Others hooked up with desperate women. After they got divorced, they snapped up the first woman they found, rebounding into relationships that ultimately failed.

Desire is critical right now; rekindle it. Write down your dreams. What would you like from your marriage? What would a great life look like for you? Take some time with these questions. I recommend you go back to this exercise in the months to come, as it will become a touchpoint for hope in your life.

Embrace the Process

The key to emerging from this season as a healthy, strong, confident man is to embrace the healing process. Nothing we've explored in this chapter happens overnight. It will take time, but the results will be worth it.

It's kind of like going up a large mountain. This past summer, my son and I drove to the top of Mount Evans in Colorado. This is the highest place you can drive in the continental United States. As we drove up the mountain road, we passed the same spots over and over again. However, each time we passed them, we found ourselves a few hundred feet higher. About 18 miles later, we stepped out onto the summit.

In the journey of recovering your heart, you'll likely pass through the same places repeatedly. When you feel desperate, turn toward confidence. When you start striving to fix everything, take a deep breath, stop, and choose to trust God. When you feel like controlling everything, let go and keep moving. When you feel despair, invite desire into your heart.

Don't be concerned when you keep passing these places. On the ascent to the top, this is normal and expected. If you embrace the moment and receive some healing each time you pass a tough place, you'll discover that you're gaining elevation. If you find yourself weeping in sadness, don't despair. Grief is a natural part of this climb. Embrace the moment, process the grief, and keep climbing.

I encourage you to take your time on the journey of recovering your heart. Linger where necessary. Every so often, you may want to pull over and take a break. Just remember to get back in your car and keep driving upward. Also, don't make the drive alone. Share it with those you trust the most: your mentor(s), brothers, and with Christ.

The drive up the mountain will take longer than expected. There will be many twists and turns. There will be times you want to quit. Eventually, though, you will find yourself at the summit. When you arrive, you'll have gained a whole new level of perspective on life. Looking down, you'll see the road that got you to the top. Things that seemed big in the moment will look much smaller from the top. You'll breathe the free air, finding yourself closer to heaven than you've ever been in your life. You'll also discover that you are stronger than before you began. You're going to need this strength for the fight.

Phase Three: The Fight

The night that she said she wanted to separate, I went to my friend John's house to spend the night. About 20 years older than me, John had also been a father figure in my life for the past 10 years. Sitting on his back porch that evening, I was shell-shocked from the bomb that had gone off in my life.

John's advice was solid: "You have to fight for this until God tells you to stop. Then, if it ends, you will be able to walk away with a good conscience and move on."

I knew he was right. I wanted to fight for my marriage to be restored, but I had no idea how hard the battle would be.

This battle will likely be the hardest one you ever fight. It doesn't seem fair to engage in conflict when you've just been dealt the biggest wound of your life, but this is where you are right now. Look at the deep wound of your wife's affair as the first salvo in a long battle.

You have an enemy. While you may not have wanted to acknowledge that there are dark forces of evil in this world, the reality is that there are. How else do you explain all of the pain on this planet?

Jesus says, "The enemy comes to steal, kill, and destroy" (John 10:10). Peter says, "The enemy prowls around like a roaring lion, seeking whom he may devour" (1 Peter 5:8).

In this section, I want to show you what's going on behind enemy lines. Then, I want to give you some practical training in how to fight.

A few of my friends play the role of "the bad guys" for a local special forces/SWAT training facility. Their stories of the mock battles with real guns will make your hair stand on end. However, they are using "simunitions" with plastic bullets instead of real ammunition, so nobody gets hurt.

What you are going through is live-action training. No one is pulling any punches here. It will be hard; there will be pain. As the trailer for the Bruce Willis movie, *Tears of the Sun*, says, "The lives of many rest in the courage of a few." Your children are depending on you. In a strange way, your wife is depending on you. Your heart is in the balance.

10: Warfare

We live in a world at war. There is a spiritual battle raging all around us. Having first entered the story in the Garden of Eden, Satan has since wreaked havoc on this earth.

One of the enemy's main targets has been marriage. He's jealous that men and women are made in the image of God. The masculine reflects God's strength; the feminine, God's tenderness. When you unite a man and woman in marriage, you get a full picture of God. The enemy absolutely hates this.

As well, the one thing humans can do that Satan can't is procreate. As the destroyer, our enemy hates that married couples can beget life. So, he will attack any marriage, good or bad.

Until now, you may have stuck your head in the sand when it came to matters of spiritual warfare. Or, perhaps you are quite aware of the enemy's tactics regarding the spiritual realm. Rest assured, though, you have probably never faced a battle as intense as the one you now face.

There are many great resources on spiritual warfare, but for the sake of our discussion right now, let me state a few realities:

You have an enemy; he is known as the devil or Satan.

There exists a kingdom of darkness. Paul gives us some insight in Ephesians 6:12: "For we wrestle not against flesh and blood, but against principalities, against powers, against the rulers of the darkness of this world, against spiritual wickedness in high places."

Jesus says that the enemy is a thief who comes to "steal, kill, and destroy."[12] There are forces of evil and they are set against you and your family. If you don't have a relationship with Jesus, it's time to change that. If you do have a relationship with Jesus, you may need to move from being a passive follower to a proactive warrior.

You were built to be a warrior. Up to this point in your life, you may not have seen yourself as a warrior. However, when you found out your wife was cheating, putting your marriage and family at risk, I'm willing to bet you felt something rise up inside you. Something inside you wanted to fight. That's the heart of a warrior.

You have a warrior's heart. Now, it's time to learn how to fight.

In the movie, *The Mask of Zorro*, the young Alejandro, played by Antonio Banderas, wants revenge for his brother's death. In a drunken stupor, he wields a sword, bent on having revenge. Don Diego, played by Anthony Hopkins, foils his attempt. As the upset Alejandro asks Don Diego why he stopped the plan of revenge, he says, "You would have fought bravely, and died quickly!"

You need to fight, but to win, you must fight with wisdom and training. In this chapter, you'll discover critical things you need to know for a successful fight.

A critical part of any battle is to know your enemy. One of the things to understand is that there are many foul spirits in his kingdom. Let's examine a few that are common when it comes to infidelity.

Spirit of Lust

Shortly after I discovered that my wife had been with another man, I began to experience deep feelings of lust. I've struggled with many things in life; however, lust has not been near the top of my list. These weren't normal feelings of simply noticing another woman. Rather, I wanted to grab any woman I saw and have sex with her.

This was not me. Several days into this, I found that I couldn't shake these feelings. I began to be concerned, so I prayed: "Father, help me. What is going on here?" In a still, small voice, I heard the reply, "There is a spirit of lust."

Despite being somewhat a novice at spiritual warfare, I did what I knew and said out loud: "Spirit of lust, I command you to go away in the name of Jesus Christ." Just like that, the lust lifted.

It was a moment of clarity. My wife had given herself over to a spirit of lust in the affair. The man she was sleeping with had too. I was still married to my wife; we had a spiritual union. Somehow, this spirit had jumped onto me.

If you begin to experience feelings of lust, first realize that these may not be you. Of course, the enemy will lie to you to get you to own these feelings, embracing the shame that goes along with them. He is a master accuser, always using shame to manipulate.

Second, tell the spirit of lust where to go: straight to hell. Jesus told his disciples that he gave them authority over demonic spirits. While this may sound radical, read the gospels and you will notice that it was almost routine for Jesus to deal with demonic forces.

For example, when he entered the area known as Gadara, on the eastern shore of the Sea of Galilee, he was confronted by a demonized man who lived in the graveyard because no one in the town could deal with him. When Jesus faced the demons in this man, they shouted at him, "What do you want with me, Jesus, Son of the Most High God? I beg you, don't torture me!" Jesus took care of the problem by telling the demons to leave the man.

Notice that these demons—and it says there were "legion"—called Jesus "Son of the Most High God." Even the demons recognize the power of Christ (see Luke 8:26-39). When you call on the name of Jesus as you encounter the enemy, they recognize and are subject to him as well.

When you run up against things that are contrary to God (such as sin or evil), it may or may not be demonic. You might have heard the expression, "The world, the flesh, or the devil." This means the obstacle you are facing might be demonic, or it might also just be an aspect of the fallen world we live in. A third option is that it is just plain old sinful flesh.

Sometimes, in other words, the devil gets credit for simple human rebelliousness. However, in all three of these obstacles—the world, the flesh, or the devil—there is one powerful solution: calling on the name of Jesus to overcome that entity standing between you and victory.

When I use the expression "the spirit of…", I am referring specifically to an actual demon that will attack you in this particular area (e.g., lust, despair, etc.). However, know that the attack you are experiencing could also have its source in the world or the flesh. In all cases, though, the enemy will try to take advantage of your misfortune.

What you need to say when you feel overpowered by lust is simple: "In the name and authority of Jesus Christ, I command the spirit of lust to go away. I send you to the cross of Jesus for your judgement. You have no authority here."

The next thing I recommend is to put the cross of Christ between you and your wife. She's messing with some dangerous forces that you don't need accessing your life. So, you might say, "I put the cross of Christ between me and my wife and all of her warfare. I forbid any of the warfare to pass between us. Only the love of Christ is allowed to pass."

The enemy is relentless, though, and won't give up easily. So, when he tries to come back, remind him that he has no authority and send the spirit of lust packing in the name of Jesus.

Here's a word of warning. If you are actively involved in pornography or fantasy, you are inviting a spirit of lust into your life. This won't help you, your wife, or your children. Once you start to see this as part of the warfare leveled against you, it puts things in a different perspective. If you continue in this behavior, you will get hammered.

What do you do? You must repent. That's a churchy word that simply means to turn—turn away from it. Turn toward God. As discussed earlier, look for the answers to your questions "Am I loved and do I have what it takes?" from God instead of women. Your wife couldn't answer these questions for you, and neither can the exploited women strung out on drugs who star in porn videos.

Spirit of Addiction

You may find this hard to believe, but right now, your wife hates herself. She hates what she is doing, how it is affecting her kids, and how it's affecting your marriage.

Yet, she continues because an affair is like an addiction. It actually pushes the same hormone buttons as drugs like cocaine. You get the high, then there is terrible shame and guilt. To numb these feelings, you go back for more. This is the proverbial vicious cycle. She may also be using alcohol or drugs to numb her guilt, which can lead to additional addictions.

Addictions operate at every level of one's being. Physically, the release of chemicals like dopamine causes a craving for more. Emotionally, the feelings of euphoria drive a longing for more. Spiritually, the sense of being alive and free, as false as it may be, creates a desire for more.

The spirit of addiction, thus, lies, saying, "If you don't have this, you will be in pain; or worse, you will die."

This is a trap. If she has a spirit of addiction, it will likely come after you as well. Your heart has been broken. Now the temptation is to turn to alcohol and drugs to numb the pain, but you put yourself at great risk, especially with the spirit of addiction also operating in your wife's life.

The problem with trying to relieve pain through substance abuse is that it doesn't actually deal with the pain. In reality, the addiction makes it worse. Instead of numbing the pain, you need to process it. Your heart has been wounded, and your marriage has been assaulted. Grieve for it, and bring it to God.

When you hear the voice saying, "You need this to numb the pain," say, "No! Instead, I choose to process the grief." Just as you took authority over the spirit of lust, take similar authority over the spirit of addiction.

Spirit of Self-Hatred

Your wife may look good on the outside now, but inevitably she will feel tremendous self-hatred for what she is doing to you, your kids, and possibly the family of the man with whom she is sleeping.

The spirit of self-hatred is brutal. It piles on with shame saying, "You are worthless." This spirit likes to assign blame. It says that, "All of this is your fault. If you weren't such a terrible husband and such an unlovable human being, she would still be here."

Ultimately, this spirit of self-hatred wants you to agree that you are fundamentally flawed. It says that you're not worthy of anything, especially the love of a woman.

One thing that clearly identifies a spirit of self-hatred is that it encourages you to only see your faults, rather than experience repentance. While the Spirit of God might bring *conviction* that would lead to change, the spirit of self-hatred brings *condemnation* that says, "You're such a piece of crap. You can't change this. It's already messed up. So, you might as well continue."

When you hear the internal voice that says, "I'm so bad at this. It's all my fault," you need to be open to the possibility that a spirit of self-hatred is involved. When you feel an overwhelming sense of condemnation and you hear the voice that says, "The marriage vows have been broken, so you might as well do the same," chances are the spirit of self-hatred is coming after you as well.

Spirit of Heaviness

The spirit of self-hatred breeds deep feelings of shame. This opens the door for a spirit of heaviness, which leads to depression. Marked by a deep feeling of hopelessness, it's like a heavy cloud descends on you.

The spirit of heaviness' ultimate goal is suicide. It wants to convince you that things will never change, they will only get worse, and your best option is to end it all.

Your wife has likely opened the door wide open to this spirit. With the self-hatred bred by her actions and their impact, she likely feels deep shame. While she may not express this to you, in the quiet moments between the highs of her affair, she feels deep depression.

Granted, what you are going through already is profoundly sad. However, when the spirit of heaviness comes into the picture, sadness goes to the next level.

During the separation, I felt a deep depression. Of course, some of this is natural and necessary as you grieve the loss of the marriage. However, at times it seemed way out of proportion—like my life was going to end. Looking back, I suspect the spirit of heaviness was involved. She had given in to this spirit and it had affected me.

When the Bible says the thief comes to "steal, kill, and destroy", it means just that. The spirit of heaviness is dangerous.

Have you noticed thoughts of suicide? Beware of the spirit of heaviness. Just as the other spirits that your wife has given access to will impact you, so too will the spirit of heaviness.

Spirit of Jealousy

While the spirits we have discussed so far come from your wife, this spirit originates from the man with whom she is having an affair. Are you jealous of him? Of course. However, set that aside for a moment and consider what may be happening here.

In a twisted way, the man she is cheating with is likely jealous of you. After all, even though he's sleeping with your wife, you are the one married to her. You have what he wants.

One day, I learned through back channels that the man my wife was having an affair with not only wanted her, he also wanted my son and my house! Essentially, he was jealous of my life and wanted it for himself.

The spirit of jealousy operates in stealth mode because it is a natural human emotion. It will also feel all-consuming. Ultimately, the goal of the spirit of jealousy is murder. Watch any crime show. What's the motive behind murder? Most often, it's a crime of passion.

You may be a fine upstanding citizen who has never considered killing anyone. Now, you find yourself not just angry at the situation, but seriously contemplating murder. Watch out; there may be a spirit of jealousy involved. It may have come from the other guy, and is now affecting you.

What do you do? Once again, take authority! "I send this spirit of jealousy to the cross of Christ for judgement." Then, ask the Father what he would like to give you in its place. Ask him to help you deal with the emotions of jealousy.

Dealing with the Warfare

While the idea of an unseen realm of evil may be new to you, I'm sure you can agree that there seem to be dark forces working against you. Even if this seems unlikely, I challenge you to be open to the possibility of this reality. What if there actually are foul spirits working against you? Wouldn't you want to deal with them?

The good news is that in Christ you have the authority to deal with this warfare. Jesus told his disciples, "Look, I have given you authority over all the power of the enemy, and you can walk among snakes and scorpions and crush them. Nothing will injure you." (Luke 19:10)

Here's the problem with the current situation. When you get married, you become one flesh and one spirit with your spouse. While this is very helpful inside marriage, it can become extremely dangerous when one spouse is cheating. In essence, due to your union with her, the foul spirits that she invited into her life now have access to you.

From one perspective, this is good news since not everything you are thinking and feeling is really yours. The spirit of lust may be driving thoughts that you don't normally have. The spirit of self-hatred may be piling on with thoughts about how terrible you are and how you caused the affair. The spirit of heaviness may be encouraging your depression and suggesting suicide. The spirit of jealousy may be dumping gasoline on the fire of what would be normal levels of jealousy, inciting you to contemplate murder.

In response, place the cross of Christ between you and her. Remember, you have authority in Christ. You might say: "I put the cross of Christ between my wife and me. I forbid any of her warfare to affect me. May only the love of Christ flow between us." If you have children, add them to that prayer as well.

This step of authority will feel so freeing in and of itself. It will likely be something you need to do many times. Foul spirits are ruthless; they need to be put in their place. As long as you are married, the spiritual union is in place between you and your wife. So, if you are still married and she's cheating, you are at risk.

Once you've put the cross of Christ between you and her warfare, ask Jesus for the truth. The good thing about recognizing the particular evil set against you and your family is that you begin to know what you're up against. You get the intel needed in order to fight.

Your wife has permitted entry to these foul spirits based on her sinful actions. In essence, her infidelity has opened up strongholds that allow the enemy to set up camp in your life. One way that he'll attempt to establish his authority is by getting you to agree with his lies.

The enemy has a spin on every situation. For example, when your wife cheats, the spirit of lust will tell you that the marriage vows are broken and the marriage bed is no longer pure, so you now have the right to do whatever you want sexually. Can you see how that could lead to behaviors that might radically damage any future hopes for your marriage?

The spirit of addiction might say that you can't handle the pain of this situation and you need to numb it with alcohol or pills. Maybe the spirit of heaviness says that not only are you depressed, but that you will always be so. The spirit of jealousy might build on your natural anger, influencing you to kill the guy who's with your wife. Agreeing with any of these interpretations will have dangerous long-term effects on you and your family.

Instead, what if you could identify and break these agreements? Ask God to reveal them; then, write them down. Your list might look something like this:

- Since she cheated, I have the right to sleep with other women.
- I'm not getting laid, so I have the right to indulge in porn.
- I will always be depressed.
- I will never get over this.
- I need something to take the edge off of this pain.
- I deserve to get drunk.
- I have the right to be angry.
- I could murder that guy.

Once you've made your list, break the agreements. This process is very simple, but you need to say it out loud because your words have authority. For example, "I break the agreement that I have the right to sleep with other women."

Next, ask God for the truth. If the enemy has spin, don't you think that Father God who loves you will have an interpretation as well?

This is where things get good. Write down what you hear in your heart. These will be words of affirmation, love, and truth. They'll also be profoundly helpful to you as you fight for your heart, your children's hearts, and your wife.

11: What Led Her to Cheat

This will be a difficult chapter. However, I challenge you to read it because as you fight for your wife, you need to understand what is happening in her heart. First, we'll explore what may have led her to cheat. Then, we'll discuss how she is now trapped. Finally, we'll explore the dynamics of her predicament.

Remember that while all women share similar traits, each one has a different story. Your wife's heart has been shaped by the story of her life. It includes how she was raised, how she was loved—or not—by her dad, and wounds she has taken from other men. It also includes where she is on her journey. Are there babies and young kids at home or is the nest empty? Is she carrying the grief of a miscarriage? Are there pressures at work or is she getting accolades for a job well done? Consider these questions to get a clearer picture of where she is today.

What May Have Led Her to Cheat

If she's like most women, chances are she's given you all kinds of reasons why she left:

- "I need some space."
- "I don't feel like I know who you are any more."
- "I feel trapped."

You've racked your brain trying to figure out what you did wrong and what you could have done differently. However, there are some common reasons why women cheat. Understanding these reasons and the benefits women receive from cheating will help you in the fight.

I'm not saying she is justified in her actions; rather, if you can understand what she thinks and feels, along with the related consequences, you have a better chance to win her heart.

Ultimately, each of the reasons to cheat outlined below are based on legitimate feelings that many women experience. The difference here is that your wife has bought into the lie that having an affair will make these problems go away, or at least bring some relief. Let's explore each of these.

She Felt Trapped; Now She Feels Free

Women can easily find themselves in a place where they feel trapped. They feel confined by their marriage. Even more so, they may feel trapped as a mother, or in a job they don't like.

Women feel tremendous pressure in today's world. This is especially true for Christian women. They are told to be attentive to their families, carrying the burden of managing a household and all that requires. They are told to be super-moms. They are told that they need to be involved in the church. These demands become heavy weights of expectation stacked onto their lives.

The message of the world bristles against the biblical picture of what it means to be a woman, telling them, "You are trapped." The prevailing belief of our society is that marriage is restrictive.

People are voting with their feet. Statistics show that less than 50% of adults in the United States are married. Television shows, movies, and books fuel the fire with stories of women choosing to be free in their relationships and sexuality.

While the empowerment of women over the past century has been necessary and good, part of the message is, "You can do life on your own." If you feel trapped, take action to escape.

The affair makes a false promise of freedom. The lie she has bought into says that her best bet to feel free is to make independent choices. So, she's choosing love, happiness, and independence. These choices are dangerous and have devastating consequences for everyone involved.

She Felt Unknown; Now She Feels Understood

The second dynamic that may have led to her cheating is that she feels unknown. Nobody really knows her true heart. She feels invisible and unheard.

As we discussed earlier, men have a core question: "Do I have what it takes?"

Women also have a core question: "Do you see me?" From her earliest childhood days all the way through womanhood, she spends her life trying to be lovely. She wants to be seen, appreciated, and understood.

Consider the television shows and novels that women love. They like stories where they get to know the characters intimately. They want to know the details of each character's story to understand what made them the person that they are.

Ask most women if they feel truly understood by their husband and the answer will likely be no. In the rut of daily life and the monotony of a marriage it's easy for a woman to feel lost. This crushes the core desire of a woman's heart to be truly known, pursued, and delighted in.

The affair makes her feel understood. The new man is listening to her heart. He's fascinated by her—or at least pretending to be. They are having long conversations. He's asking questions.

This is where we misunderstand the motives of our wives. As men, if we have an affair, it's often a mixture of unfulfilled sexual drive and our core desire to see if we "have what it takes." For most men, the affair is a conquest born out of an unfulfilled longing for adventure. For women, the affair is primarily emotional, born from their true drive to be known.

She Felt Lonely; Now She Feels Companionship

The core fear of a woman is that she will be abandoned. Even if she is in a marriage with a husband who is committed to her and surrounded by kids who think she hung the moon, there is still something inside her that says, *They could leave and I would be abandoned.*

The loneliness of our culture compounds a woman's fear of abandonment. We live in the most isolated society in history. While we are hyper-connected to each other through the Internet, online connections feel shallow.

Social media sites only make the situation worse. Not only do they give a false sense of connection, they also fuel envy of other people's seemingly perfect lives while encouraging you to present a false self to the world.

Men may not like feeling alone, but they can live with it. For many women, feeling alone pushes the button of their deepest and darkest fear of abandonment. The affair, thus, promises to remove some of her loneliness. She has a companion who his pursuing her.

Here's the catch. At some point when the endorphin high wears off of the new relationship, she'll come to her senses and realize that if the guy she is with would pursue her as a married woman, he will likely pursue someone else.

Ironically, this realization can make her feel lonely, which can drive her further into the affair or, if the guy she is cheating with moves on, into the arms of the next man.

She Felt Bored; Now She Feels Excitement

Daily life can be boring, especially for a married woman with children.

Consider the monotony of her daily routine: Get the kids ready for school. Make lunch. Rush to work. Pick up the kids. Scramble to make dinner. Put the kids to bed. Try to grab a few minutes of peace. Go to sleep knowing you'll have to do it all over again tomorrow. On the weekends, do laundry, go to soccer games, and clean the house.

If your wife stays home with babies, her routine might be even duller, not to mention exhausting. If you're at work all the time or traveling, she spends her days and evenings alone, bored and lonely. If she's an empty nester, no longer responsible for the busy life of a parent, she can be bored combined with a loss of purpose.

All these reasons make her vulnerable to an affair.

The affair offers excitement and breaks her out of her routine. Even during her routine, the affair gives her something to fantasize about and look forward to. The hidden aspect of the affair and the risk of being caught also relieves boredom.

Just as every sin begins with the seed of thought, an affair usually starts as a fantasy that germinates in the soil of boredom. It's watered and nurtured by TV shows, movies, magazines, social media, and novels that showcase a better life.

In the months leading up to my wife's affair, I noticed that she started consuming *People* magazine and watching the HBO series, *Sex and the City*. I can see now how this watered the seeds of fantasy that were planted in the soil of boredom.

She Felt Ugly; Now She Feels Attractive

It doesn't matter if she has a modeling contract: hang out with a group of women and you find that most feel insecure about how they look. Our culture puts tremendous pressure on women to not only be beautiful, but to be perfect.

Let's be honest, having a few kids and getting older means that you don't look like you're in your twenties anymore. For today's woman, this is a problem to be solved, and a reason to hate yourself.

The affair makes her feel beautiful. Being noticed by a new man gives her exactly what she wants: to feel attractive.

One thing I've noticed about women who are getting ready to have an affair is that they become obsessed with their bodies. After years of not seeming to care about how they look, they'll hire a personal trainer, hit the tanning bed, and change their eating habits. As a husband, you may be happy that she's finally motivated to get in shape. Sadly, some women are not doing this for their husbands, but to feel attractive for the other man.

She Felt Unloved; Now She Feels Love

Every woman wants to feel loved. Right now, she doesn't feel loved. Yes, I'm confident that you love her. Otherwise, you wouldn't care enough to make it this far into the book. What I'm saying is that she doesn't *feel* it.

There are many reasons why she might not feel your love. Maybe you're not speaking her love language. In the book, *Five Love Languages,* Gary Chapman talks about the five love languages:

- Words of Affirmation
- Acts of Service
- Physical Touch
- Receiving Gifts
- Quality Time

Chances are that your love language is different from hers. If you try to communicate your love to her in your love language, it's like you're speaking French to a girl raised in Seattle. She may understand a few words here and there, but she isn't going to receive the full communication.

She may not be receiving your love because of a thick shell of resentment. Marriage is hard, requiring much forgiveness and grace. After years of unforgiveness toward you, her heart may have developed a protective layer.

As Bruce Springsteen so eloquently says, "Everybody has a hungry heart." The affair offers her a feeling of love for her hungry heart. Whether or not that love is genuine is irrelevant at this point.

She Felt Controlled; Now She Feels Free

Unfortunately, when you ask many women how they feel about their husbands, they say they feel controlled by them. Over time, this builds resentment.

In the early years of my adulthood (also the early years of my marriage), fear was my constant companion as a man. I was afraid I didn't have what it took to be successful at work or as a husband. All of the pressures of life created a fear of failure and drove me to try to control my world.

At the same time, I was a member of a church. The message I heard as a man was that I needed to control myself or sinful desires could burn out of control and ruin my life. I figured that if I could control my life, I could then avoid pain.

During one of the sessions with my counselor, she said, "When you try to control your own life, other people around you feel controlled."

I had no idea. I thought that the control I was trying to exercise over my own life was making other's lives better. Instead, I discovered that my wife felt controlled by me. This tight grip was suffocating her.

Since then, I discovered that the control I thought I had over my life was at best an illusion. Instead, I'm learning to walk a path of trust and surrender, holding on to people and things much more loosely. I'm finding out that I can trust my Father God with my life. I'm also learning that while there a few things in my life that I can directly affect, most of life is beyond my control. The good news is that, led by the Holy Spirit, I have what it takes to handle the things that happen.

I'm also learning that the struggle in my life is not against "flesh and blood, but against the unseen powers of the dark world,"[14] as Paul says. The battle is not to control those closest to me, but rather to fight against the enemy on behalf of my family.

She Felt Wounded; Now She Feels Some Relief

Life deals brutal blows to every human being. We're all walking around emotionally wounded from events in our past. Chances are your wife has been wounded in many ways by neglectful or abusive parents, friends, and ex-boyfriends. She's also been wounded by you.

Over the years, many women develop deeply wounded, unhealed hearts. When someone has been physically, emotionally, or sexually abused, they will usually form a layer of self-protection toward the opposite sex. If she was abused or neglected, she may have created a protective barrier around her heart that keeps your love from connecting with her.

Wounds come with pain. For unhealed wounds that have been around for years—even decades—this pain becomes chronic and demands attention.

Consider your wife's story. Imagine the combined effect of the emotional pain related to her wounds. Now, overlay her history on your marriage up until today. Do you see a pattern? Did she ever receive the healing she needed from her past in order to walk functionally in the present?

When you experience emotional pain, there are two potential solutions: you can pursue healing or you can medicate. Even if a woman realizes the source of their emotional pain, the path of healing can be a long journey. Instead, most women—well, most *people*—choose self-medication or distractions.

A good woman can begin with pouring themselves into mothering, working, or hobbies. They may go down the path of self-improvement or its close cousin, religion. (I use the word "religion" here to mean doing things for God out of a sense of having to earn his favor rather than accept his grace.) When these things fail to relieve the pain, they find themselves looking for more.

The affair offers relief from the pain; it's like a drug. In fact, as we'll explore in the next section, the rush of chemicals is similar to the experience of a drug addict.

What's Going on in Your Wife's Heart?

So far in this chapter, you've seen some common categories for what happens in the heart of a woman that might lead her to cheat. Every woman's story is different. Prayerfully ask God to give you insight into her heart. In addition to understanding what may have caused the affair, you need to understand where she is right now. She may have *felt* trapped before the affair, but now that she is in one, she really *is* trapped. Next, we will explore the predicament in which she finds herself.

She is Deceived

At this point, some of the reasons your wife cheated are clearer. The temptation now is to confront her with truth and reality, hoping she will see the light and come back to her family.

That would be a great idea except for one big problem: she is deceived. She has willingly bought into the lie that the affair will give her the things she wants. She's bought in physically and emotionally with the rush of endorphins that come from new love. Also, she's engaged in willful sin, opening the door to spiritual attack.

The problem with being deceived is simple: you cannot see things through an objective lens. Reality has been reframed for you. Deception is like bad breath: we are the last one to realize that we have it.

No amount of logic will help. In fact, the more you reason with her, the more likely she will double down. Your efforts to bring some sense to her will feel like control. This will reinforce her belief that she is trapped, unknown, lonely, and unloved.

She is Deceitful

In addition to being deceived, she has also had to become a deceiver. Affairs happen in secret. The affair has required her to lie and hide. For some time, she has been living two lives.

You're not the only person she's lied to. The coverup has extended to your children, extended family, and friends. To pull off the affair, she has needed to deceive many other people as well.

She is Ashamed

If she does miraculously overcome being deceived for a moment to see reality, another dynamic appears: shame. When she sees how her actions have hurt you and her children, her heart will be flooded with shame. The enemy absolutely loves this.

There is a big difference between conviction and shame. Conviction says that you did something wrong. Shame goes a step further and says that in addition to *doing* something wrong, there *is* something wrong with you. Shame says you are deeply flawed as a human being. Its message is that you are broken and irredeemable.

The enemy wants your cooperation in shaming here. You may want to say things like, "I can't believe what you are doing to our children. What kind of person would do something this terrible?" Your attempts to shame your wife may feel good in the moment. However, as much as you want to say things like this to her, hoping that it will snap her out of her deception, the reality is that you are only cooperating with the enemy in piling on shame.

Remember, the Bible says that it's the "kindness of God that leads us toward repentance" (Romans 2:4). Even if you don't see it, she already feels a lot of shame. Piling more on top of what she already feels actually puts you with her enemy. It will not help you fight for her heart.

No human being can endure the pain of shame for long. At some point, they will either seek relief to numb it, or pursue genuine healing.

She is Addicted

Your wife is addicted. The same addictive characteristics of drugs also exist in the emotional rush of an affair.

Dr. Scott Haltzman, author of *The Secrets of Surviving Infidelity*, explains the addictive aspects of an affair:

When most people think of infidelity, they don't think of injecting heroin or smoking crack cocaine. They ought to, because the behavior that takes place during an affair mimics exactly the behavior of a drug addict. ("Flame Addiction": The Neuroscience of Infidelity, *Brain World Magazine*)

When a person begins to be attracted to someone else, a set of chemical and hormonal changes are set into motion. During the first stages of the affair, adrenaline-like norepinephrine literally takes her breath away. This rush of new love is like drinking a Red Bull for your emotions; it feels great.

When they are apart, serotonin drops. This is the chemical in antidepressants. When this happens, she feels a sense of emptiness when she is away from the other man. This fuels an obsession with him. *Web*MD says, "Because low serotonin in the brain is related to obsessive disorder, some scientists think low serotonin is a likely explanation for the way people in love obsess about their beloved." (Martin Downs, "Timeline of a Love Affair," *Web*MD)

The affair also spikes dopamine, the feel-good reward chemical. Dopamine floods into the bloodstream with the rush of new love. This is the same type of response a cocaine user feels. When it's gone, her body craves more. According to *Web*MD, "The downside of high dopamine is anxiety, restlessness, and emotional volatility." Much like a drug user, dopamine will cloud her judgement.

While this addiction does not excuse her behavior, it can help you understand it better. Much like a drug addict needs another hit, your wife now craves the affair. However, she's not really addicted to the other man, but rather to all of the physical and emotional feelings that come from infidelity.

She is Defiant

To get to where she is in the affair, she has had to shut off her conscience. You don't have to tell her what she's doing is wrong. She knows that adultery is sinful. She knows she has violated her vows and that a divorce will hurt her kids. Despite all of this, she's chosen the affair anyway.

This state requires a defiant attitude. It's a heart that says, *I know this is wrong, but I don't care anymore.* This comes with an arrogance and self-entitlement that says, *I deserve to feel good and I'm going to do whatever I want.*

She certainly doesn't care what you think (or won't admit that she does). While parts of her heart may have softened toward the other man, her heart toward you and God has become hard.

She is in Spiritual Bondage

When she committed adultery, she didn't just open her life to another man, she opened the door to the enemy. As we discussed earlier, the enemy of her soul will take full advantage of the doors she has opened. Spirits of adultery, lust, and fornication have been invited into her life by her actions. Like any sin, the immediate rush of pleasure feels good, but the aftermath comes with a deep bondage.

Previously, we discussed the importance of fighting against these foul spirits. As we now consider the state of your wife's heart, I want you to think how spiritual bondage might be affecting her heart.

Jesus calls the enemy the Father of Lies. (John 8:44) As you might expect, he is lying to her. There is a constant stream of falsehood being offered to her: "You deserve this." "If your heart is for this other man, you must follow it." "It's not that wrong. Everyone is doing this." Much like the enemy's first lie in the Garden of Eden, he's saying, "If you do this, you will not surely die." If she's continuing in the affair, that means she's buying into most of these lies.

The enemy is also known as the Accuser. (Revelation 12:10) When he's not feeding you lies, he's serving up accusations: "You're a whore." "You're destroying your family." "You are unredeemable." "Your husband could never love you again because of this. In fact, you're unlovable as a woman. God could never love you again either."

The enemy's cycle of lies and accusations become like a rope wrapped around her life. This is a hard place to live.

She is in a Relational Mess

She now finds herself in the center of a relational mess. Practically, she feels some level of commitment to keep her family together. However, she knows she has done severe damage to the marriage.

At the same time, she feels drawn to another man. The challenge here is that she knows in the back of her mind that a cheater will likely cheat. If the other man has disrespected the boundary of marriage to cheat with her, he likely will do the same again.

This is what we call a relational mess. She's caught between desiring the love of a man and the security of her marriage relationship. She has the rush of intense feelings with her new lover, but she had a level of security with you.

If she continues with the affair, at some point she knows that divorce is imminent. Even though nobody can know how painful a divorce can be before they go through it, at minimum she knows it will be messy.

If she decides to return to you, she has to deal with the pain of breaking from her new love. Whether you like this reality or not, in her mind this will cause much grief, as she has likely given large parts of her heart to this new man.

At the same time as she's grieving, she'd need the humility to come back to you. Instead of the roses and butterflies of the affair, she knows that restoring a relationship with you will require a lot of hard work.

If children are involved, at some point she faces the relational dynamics of telling the children that their parents are getting divorced. No woman wants to break this news to their children. Even if she is planning to leave you and move on, she'll delay this conversation as long as possible because of the pain she knows it will cause them.

Then there is the extended family and your network of friends. Each one of these people who are close to both her and you present another layer of relational complexity should the affair become public and she decides to move on.

Add all this up and you can see that she has created the ultimate relational dilemma full of hard choices. Remember, right now in her life, she doesn't want hard choices; she wants to feel free, excited, beautiful, and loved. Every one of these relational choices makes her feel the exact opposite.

She is Defensive

How do you feel when you get backed into a corner? What about when your deepest secrets are exposed or you get caught red-handed? You feel very defensive. You also get angry. And guess what? *No one*, when they are angry, can be wrong.

She has done things that she would be embarrassed for most of her circle of family and friends to know about. In the process, she has been living two lives, creating a false front not only to you, but many other people around her. All of this has required her to lie and hide.

Throughout the affair, the enemy have whispered to her things like, "You deserve this." The world has backed this up with a popular culture that portrays infidelity as a normal part of life and relationships. Most likely, she has absorbed all of this as truth since the natural tendency of people is to look for things to validate their choices. Thus, she will be defensive when she is exposed and her moral choices are challenged.

She is Ready to Shift Blame

In this defensive posture, she will likely turn things back on you. From her perspective, she's angry that you didn't meet her needs, and now she finds herself in this big mess.

If you treated your wife terribly, abusing her verbally or physically, she has a right to be angry at you. You know this in your heart. If you simply ignored her needs, being emotionally absent from the relationship, she's angry because these wounds build up over time, breeding resentment.

Regardless of whether your poor treatment was part of what drove her away, she's now in a big pickle. She doesn't want to take the blame for her choices. So, you'll likely find her shifting blame to you.

Most men hear things like, "If you had loved me better, I wouldn't have needed to have an affair."

During my wife's affair, we went to counseling together a few times. Sitting in the counselor's office, I poured my heart out, sharing how much I truly loved her. As I shared this, she said, "Had I known that you cared this much, maybe I wouldn't be in this situation—but now it's too late since I've given my heart to someone else."

Do you hear the shift of blame in these words? She was basically saying, "You caused me to do this!"

When I heard this, I grabbed onto it. After all, no husband is perfect. While I had been faithful to her and to God throughout our marriage, I could definitely see areas where I had neglected her. In my desperation, I wanted to take the blame she was assigning me and use it to motivate me to fix the marriage.

Here's the challenge: deep inside, part of you wants to take the blame for her cheating. Why? Because if your negative actions caused the affair, it gives you hope that your positive actions and commitment to work on the marriage could return you to the life you so desperately miss.

You did not cause your wife to have an affair. The way you treated her may have contributed to her loneliness, boredom, or woundedness, but she is the one who decided to ignore her conscience and break the vows. It's your choice as to whether or not you will take the blame.

She is Scared

Fear is a constant companion for her now. There are a lot of "what ifs" running through her head.

One of the core desires of a woman's heart is for security. The choices she has made have removed most of her security. Even if your marriage wasn't great, it was something that she could depend on. Now, that is in jeopardy.

She loves this new man (or thinks she does). However, every woman knows that the man who would cheat with her will likely leave her for the next woman. So, while she may be getting a high out of the affair, she's left without any security because of this lingering fear.

Beyond the relationship insecurity are the realities of daily life. How can I pay the bills? Where will I live? Will my income be enough? What if I lose my job? So, while she has pursued the relationship to fulfill her core need to be loved and pursued, she finds herself now lacking in the core need to be financially secure.

She Feels Despair

All of this adds up to intense feelings of despair. Webster defines despair as, "The complete loss or absence of hope."

Try to put your anger aside for a few moments and enter into her world. She has created a big mess. When the emotional high of new love wears off, she will find herself wrestling with many dark emotions. She's disrupted her life, your life, and her kids' lives.

After what she's done, returning to you seems nearly impossible—even if that becomes her preference. Yet, the fear of her new lover leaving her and trying to do life on her own seems like a hard path. In this place, it feels like there are no good choices.

This is where despair sets in. Dark feelings of hopelessness flood her mind. Anxiety, depression, and fear become regular companions. She may be feeling suicidal. What does someone do when they feel intense emotions like this? They try to numb the pain and silence the noise.

How does she do this? As someone who has become addicted to the feelings of the affair, that's probably where she will go for relief. If she's still in the affair, the feelings of despair will likely drive her back into the arms of the other man. If that affair is over, there's a good chance she'll pursue yet another man.

Where is Your Wife's Heart?

If you want to fight for your wife's heart and your marriage, you need to understand where she is. If not, you'll end up doing things that drive her further away. Yes, it's probably brutally painful to try to empathize with your wife right now, but it's important to understand where she's coming from. Remember, there's a big difference between understanding a person's behaviors and condoning them.

Get out a piece of paper or a journal and take some notes. Do this prayerfully—ask God to give you insight into her heart. After all, he made women and he knows your wife very well. The things you see here will help you fight for your wife's heart and your marriage.

12: Strategies for the Fight

In *The Return of the King*, the final installment in J. R. R. Tolkien's *The Lord of the Rings* trilogy, King Théoden is faced with the reality that the enemy is coming for his kingdom. Being a prudent and responsible man, when challenged to engage the enemy, he says, "I will not risk open war." To that, Strider, also known as Aragorn the returning king, says, "Open war is upon you whether you would risk it or not."

Open war is upon you. If you are ready to fight, this chapter will give you advice to formulate your battle plan. First, we'll survey the players involved. Next, we'll explore some ground rules. Then, we'll formulate a strategy.

Who is Involved?

There are multiple players on this battlefield. You need to understand each one to fully appreciate the dynamics of the battle.

The Enemy

Earlier, we established that you have an enemy. This adds a critical dynamic to the fight. Paul says, "For we do not wrestle against flesh and blood, but against principalities, against powers, against the rulers of the darkness of this age, against spiritual hosts of wickedness in the heavenly places."[19]

I don't presume to understand everything about this reality, but suffice it to say that there are dark forces at work in the service of Satan's mission to "steal, kill, and destroy"(John 10:10) your life.

As the Father of Lies, the enemy's primary strategy is psychological warfare. He's a master spin doctor with an interpretation of every event and conversation. He works hard to get you to agree with his interpretation of reality. Given your wife's actions, it's obvious that he has served up lies and she has swallowed the bait.

- The enemy' s lies are powerful and have with elements of truth. In the current context, he likely has all kinds of things to say about you as a man:
- "You are weak. No wonder she chose another man over you."
- "You'll never get over your anger problem."
- "This is all your fault."
- You'll never get her back."
- "You're such a failure."

"Your life is going to be lonely, dark, and hopeless."

The enemy wants you to say in your heart, *Yes, that really is true.* Thus, as you agree with his lies, you begin to create a new reality. That new reality becomes a prison that holds back areas of your life.

You then begin to echo the enemy's statements describing your life. They become your beliefs about yourself, and you whisper them inwardly:

I am a weak man. This is why she left me.

I will never overcome my anger issues.

This really is my fault.

I'll never get her back.

I am a failure.

The rest of my life will be lonely, dark, and hopeless.

The net effect of this is inaction, self-doubt, fear, and self-hatred.

To counteract these lies, your best strategy is to ask God to show you the truth. Ask him to reveal any agreements that you have made. When you discover one, break it! Simply say out loud:

- "I break the agreement that I'm a weak man!"
- "I break the agreement that I'm not a real man!"
- "I break the agreement that this is all my fault!"
- "I break the agreement that I'll never get her back!"
- "I break the agreement that I'm a failure."

However, don't stop there. In place of the lie, ask God to reveal the truth about what he thinks of you in these areas. If the enemy had a spin, God has an interpretation as well.

Listen to what you hear in your heart and write them down. These are words you need to remember to counteract the lies.

Are you wondering if God really speaks? Remember, Jesus was a clear example in this area. He says plainly, "My sheep know my voice, and I know them, and they follow me." (John 10:27) You can hear the voice of God. He will reveal truth to you!

How do you know if what you hear is from God? First, he will never say anything that contradicts his word in the Bible. For example, if you think you hear God say to go kill the man who is sleeping with your wife, then that's not the voice of God because he clearly said, "Do not murder."

Another way to know if you've heard the voice of God is to ask for confirmation. This is especially important when you have a big decision to make. When you think you've heard something from God, write it down. Then, ask for confirmation. Pay attention over the next few days and see what happens. This will be immensely helpful, giving you the peace that you have heard the voice of God and are taking a good next step.

Proverbs says, "Plans fail for lack of counsel, but with many advisers, they succeed" (Proverbs 15:22). Ask one or two highly trusted brothers or mentors to weigh what you have heard as well. You need their wisdom right now, and God loves to use trusted friends to confirm what he is already saying to us.

Your Wife

The next player we'll explore is your wife. This is where it gets tricky. By definition, as you fight for your marriage and family, you're fighting for her. Yet, in many ways, she is fighting against you. How do you reconcile this?

The first thing to realize is that you're not fighting against her. You are fighting for her heart. Deep underneath all of her wounds, lives the heart that you first fell in love with. Right now, she is not herself. Your job is to contend for her true heart and rescue the beauty trapped inside.

The Bible includes a story of a man named Hosea. In this strange story, God tells him to marry Gomer, fully knowing that she will cheat on Hosea. Over and over, she cheats on him. Over and over, Hosea fights for her and takes her back. At one point in the story, she is selling herself as a prostitute and God tells him to pay for her services to get her back.

Hosea's story does not excuse infidelity. God has plenty to say about Gomer's adultery, making a parallel to the adulterous actions of the nation of Israel. However, Hosea's pursuit of his wife gives us insight into how we can fight for our cheating wives. I love this passage in Hosea 2 about how God woos the nation of Israel back to himself, just as a husband (Hosea) woos a wayward wife (Gomer):

Therefore, I am now going to allure her; I will lead her into the wilderness and speak tenderly to her. There, I will give her back her vineyards, and will make the Valley of Achor [trouble] a door of hope. There she will respond as in the days of her youth, as in the day she came up out of Egypt. "In that day," declares the Lord, "you will call me 'my husband'; you will no longer call me 'my master.'"(Hosea 2:14-16)

To fight for your wife, you have to see her true heart beneath the pain she is inflicting. In the story above, God speaks to the nation of Israel as a husband would speak to a promiscuous wife, luring "her" (Israel) into the wilderness, and speaking tenderly to her. Similarly, God has a strategy for your wife. He loves her. He wants her to receive his forgiveness, repent, find healing, and return to your family. The main question you can ask him is, "How can I cooperate with what you are doing to restore her life?"

Everything in you wants to be angry at her. While anger is a very valid emotion, in the story of Gomer, God looks past her actions and sees her true heart. Instead of lashing out in anger, he says, "I'm going to allure her." He decides that instead of speaking words of bitterness, he will speak words of tenderness.

Could you do this? Could you see her true heart inside? Could you "allure" her and speak tenderly to her? If so, you would be cooperating with God's agenda for her life.

In this fight for your wife's heart, it's kind of like rescuing a drowning person. While they desperately want to be rescued, they will kick, scream, and wrestle against the person who's trying to save them. Similarly, your wife wants to be rescued, but she will likely fight against it the whole time.

In this battle, you must remember that you are fighting for what's deep inside your wife, not the outside actions. You do this with tenderness, not with harsh words. You allure (i.e., woo or attract) her, instead of trying to control her.

Remember, Paul says that it's the kindness of God that leads us to repentance, not his judgement. With her adultery, right now judgement feels like the right thing to deliver. True to form, Jesus recommends the opposite of what you'd expect: kindness.

I know a man whose wife was ready to file divorce papers and was treating him poorly. He also had a lot to lose in the divorce. After hearing from God, he decided to be kind to her. He began to serve her in practical ways, like putting up Christmas decorations at the house while she was gone for the weekend. Behind the scenes, he prayed for blessings and favor over her life. He committed not to fight during the divorce process. He did all of this with no expectation of anything in return.

His kindness melted her heart. Not only are they back together, but they are in love. None of this would have happened without the weapon of kindness.

The Other Man

Everything inside you wants to rip the other guy's head off. This home wrecker is taking advantage of the married woman who happens to be your wife. He's preying on her weakness. In a world full of single women, he's chosen to pursue someone who is off limits and actively violating the sacred covenant of marriage. He's like a poacher who kills exotic game for the thrill of breaking the law.

What drives a man to stoop this low? Earlier, we established that every man has two core questions: "Do I have what it takes?" and "Am I loved?" We need to get these questions answered by somebody. If they don't get answered by our heavenly father, our earthly dad, or by other men, we will go to women for the answers.

Ultimately, these questions can only fully be answered by God. If they remain unanswered, they drive men to do things that seem unconscionable. It doesn't matter if the man is a homeless drunk or a successful business executive; if he doesn't have good answers to these questions, his hunger will drive him.

I know a guy who was a respected men's leader in his church and a pillar in the local business community. He was involved in Christian mission work and raised money for non-profits. In many ways, he was the last person you would expect to pursue an affair.

Yet, that's exactly what happened. He walked away from all of it, surrendering his reputation. In one sense, everyone was left totally puzzled. However, from the perspective of the two questions, it appears now to me that most of the seemingly righteous efforts in his life to be successful were attempts to get these questions answered outside of God. When that didn't make him feel loved or validated, he pursued a woman.

If a man craves answers to his two core questions, an affair seems like a great choice because you get a bonus with each answer. Regarding having what it takes, the fact that you won a woman's heart combined with her efforts to be with you say, "Yes, you have what it takes as a man." The bonus is that replacing another man to whom the woman is married gives the sense that you are better than him. So, you feel validated as a man.

The second question about being loved is answered for the adulterous man because he experiences the rush of new love driven by the hormones it releases. Add to that the adrenaline of sin done in secret, and an affair can seem like an even more powerful answer.

Here's his dilemma: all of these answers are temporary.

Recently, while having dinner at a restaurant, I saw the man who had left everything to pursue another woman. It had now been several years since the affair. She left her husband to marry this man who left his wife. Across the restaurant, I had a full view of both of them at a corner table. He seemed bored while she was rattling on expressively about something. The newness of the affair had worn off. I suspect that this man is now stuck in this marriage, wondering if he is loved and if he has what it takes. Now he has to live with the insecurity of being married to a woman he knows has cheated on her first husband. He has to wonder if she'll do it again. It would not surprise me to see him chase another woman for the answer.

The world is full of insecure men walking around looking for answers to these two big questions. It's likely that this is what is driving the sorry excuse for a man that is pursuing your wife.

Your wife's neediness and availability provided him an outlet. He doesn't love her—he only loves how she can answer his core questions. He doesn't love God (or if he does, it is buried under an avalanche of denial). If he did, he would have respect for the sanctity of marriage. While he may look confident on the outside, inside he's a weak, insecure boy looking for love and validation.

This man has given himself over to the enemy. Spirits of lust and fornication have been invited into his life. He is cooperating with the enemy's mission to steal, kill, and destroy. He is also aligned with the enemy's jealousy of women and hatred of marriage.

Your Children

If you have children, you must fight for them. Prioritizing the battle is critical. Your temptation is to focus all of your energy on saving the marriage. The battle is first for your heart. Next, it's for your children's hearts. After that, it's for your wife's heart.

The day that I discovered my wife was cheating, a wise man landed in my living room. He said, "The real battle here is not for your heart, it's for your son's heart." It certainly didn't feel like it at the time, but I knew what he was saying was true. As much as the enemy was trying to take me out, his real target was my boy.

The enemy hates children; he preys on the vulnerable. The best way to destroy someone's life is to strike while they are young. He knows the most efficient way to get this done is by attacking your marriage. If he can destroy the marriage, he can knock out the primary source of love, identity, and stability that the child needs. In turn, he can sow seeds of confusion and instability.

Your children need you right now. They need a righteous warrior to stand up and fight for them. They need stability and love.

You may not feel like you have anything to give. Emotionally, you are drained; physically, you are spent; spiritually, you are battered. How can you fight for your children when you feel so spent and empty?

Turn to the Father who wants to fight for you, just as King David did. When David was at his lowest, he said God "lifted me out of the slimy pit, out of the mud and mire; he set my feet on a rock and gave me a firm place to stand" (see Psalm 40:2). The fact is, you don't have to find the reserves by yourself—God will provide what you need for the battle.

Just as the enemy lies to you, he lies to your children. Here are some of the common ones:

This is all your fault; you need to fix it.

Your parents are going to get divorced and you'll be all alone.

You are not loved.

Your role as a father fighting for your children is to counteract these lies. First, you do this behind the scenes in prayer. Take authority over your children and let the enemy know that he does not have any power over them. Ask God to send the Holy

Spirit and his angels to guard their hearts and minds. This is especially true after you drop them off to see their mom. She has a lot of warfare happening around her. Your responsibility is to pray for their protection.

As you pray, ask God to show you the lies that the enemy is serving up to your children. Then, ask him to reveal the truth. You can take this to the next level by finding Bible verses to reinforce that truth. Then, pray specifically for your children. For example:

Father, I know the enemy has said that this is all their fault. I stand against that lie now. I ask you to reveal to them that they are loved by you, that this is not their fault, and that you are with them in all of this. Jesus, come now with your truth. Speak words of love into their hearts. Cover and protect them through all of this. As much as the enemy has tried to come against them, I ask that you protect them even more. Just as the enemy has tried to take them out, I ask that you bring additional blessing into their lives.

Don't pray alone, though, ask friends and relatives to surround your children in prayer—to literally bathe them in the protection of God's truth and love. There is power when two or more gather together in prayer, for God is there also (see Matthew 18:20).

In addition to praying for your children, speak words of love and affirmation over them. Counteract the lies. Do it tenderly. Know that as much as you are hurting, they are hurting even more. Do it when they are awake to their face, when you are driving to and from work, and from their bedside as they are sleeping.

Ground Rules for the Fight

In response to their wife's affair, most men fight for their marriage out of desperation or anger. As you heal and begin to understand where she is, you will be ready to fight from a place of knowledge. This may happen gradually: as you recover and get healthier, you will have an accelerating sense of clarity of your wife's true motives, your children's needs, and the enemy's strategy. This will help you proceed forward.

For other men going through this dark fog of pain and frustration, the tipping point comes swiftly. It's as if you are battering away at a brick wall with a sledge hammer, with little to show for your efforts. Then, suddenly on the 99th blow, you see a crack in the wall. One more mighty swing and down tumble the bricks.

I guarantee you this, though, friend: clarity and strength will come if you stay in the fight and let God take the lead.

Let God Do His Work

The first ground rule for the battle is to let God do his thing. He has a plan for restoration; your role is to cooperate.

In the story of Hosea, we see God challenging Hosea to be tender to his wife. However, in chapter two, we see God doing many other things behind the scenes. He actively opposes her choices. He says, "I will make her like a desert, turn her into a parched land, and slay her with thirst."[23] Continuing, he says, "She said, 'I will go after my lovers, who give me my food and my water, my wool and my linen, my olive oil and my drink.' Therefore, I will block her path with thorn bushes; I will wall her in so that she cannot find her way."[24]

God will actively oppose her adulterous lifestyle. While it may look like she's having a great time at your expense, the reality is that her infidelity will be likely resisted by God. In his grace and love for her, he will not allow her choices to thrive. Instead, he will lead her into the desert.

The Bible says that the wages of sin is death.[25] The fruit of your wife's cheating will be death. At some point, she will find herself in a spiritual and emotional desert, naked, thirsty, and hungry. If you want to fight for your wife, let her go, and then wait.

In the desert, he will speak tenderly to her. Right now, you may be very frustrated that your wife isn't open to both your reason and your love. That's because she hasn't arrived in the desert yet. Be patient; she will get there. At that point, your job is to cooperate with God and speak tenderly to her.

In Alcoholics Anonymous, they call this process "hitting bottom." Perhaps your wife isn't there yet, but it's not your job to help in her journey downward. Let God guide her once she does hit bottom.

Similarly, God will oppose the man with whom she is cheating. Read the words of the apostle Paul on this topic:

It is God's will that you should be sanctified: that you should avoid sexual immorality; that each of you should learn to control your own body in a way that is holy and honorable, not in passionate lust like the pagans, who do not know God; and that in this matter no one should wrong or take advantage of a brother or sister. The Lord will punish all those who commit such sins, as we told you and warned you before. For God did not call us to be impure, but to live a holy life. Therefore, anyone who rejects this instruction does not reject a human being but God.[26]

You've been taken advantage of by another man who God is actively resisting. This is a dangerous place to be, so let God do his work.

Lean Back

You want the relationship and family restored. You're reading books, going to counseling, taking care of the house, and playing super-dad. You have a very high level of willingness.

She wants out. She's given her heart over to escape what in her mind has become a prison. She's committed to navigating her life to integrate her new relationship while saving face with her kids, her family, and her friends. She also has a very high level of willingness—it's just not directed toward you or the marriage.

One day, my counselor started talking with me about this. During the separation, there was a period of time where I'd talked my wife into letting me take her to dinner once a week to discuss our relationship and our son. My counselor said, "Next time you're with your wife at dinner, try leaning forward at the table and see what happens. Then, try leaning back in your seat and let me know what the results are."

That evening at dinner, I remembered my counselor's advice. During the conversation, I leaned forward. Guess what? She leaned back. This was a perfect illustration of how I was handling the relationship. In my desperation to restore the relationship, I was the one leaning in. I had all the motivation. It left her no room.

After noticing how my whole upper body was almost halfway across the table, I intentionally leaned back in my chair. Within 30 seconds, she leaned forward. A few minutes later, I decided to see what would happen if I leaned forward again. Instinctively, she leaned back in her seat.

What I learned in that moment was powerful. When you are the one with all of the willingness, all of the effort, and all of the desire, there is no space for her to lean in. In fact, the opposite occurs. She leans back.

At this point, my advice to you may seem counterintuitive. Stop leaning forward. Stop trying so hard.

She's probably been telling you that the reason she left is all—or mostly—your fault. As men, our natural instinct is to jumping into action. We lean across the table even more. When she recoils, we climb over the table in a heroic effort to win her heart. Ironically, this pushes her back.

Why do you need to lean back? First, nothing destroys intimacy more than pressure. Your frantic efforts to fix things add more pressure to a fragile relationship.

Remember the song "Hold On Loosely" by the band 38 Special? The lyrics go, "Just hold on loosely, but don't let go. If you cling too tightly, you're gonna lose control." It's the same concept here. I'd go so far as to say that when it comes to your wife at this moment, you do need to fully let go.

Second, desperation is not attractive. Sure, you think that trying harder will make her come running back to you. That may be what she said. However, the reality is that your clingy, try-too-hard attitude is a turnoff, especially in the context of the new-love fantasy world she's living in.

Third, and most important, when you are the one doing all of the work to restore the relationship and support the family, she doesn't have to do anything. Yet she's the one who needs to do some work.

For any healing to occur, you need to back off and create some space. Here are a few basics:

Don't reply to her texts within 10 seconds.

She may be always on your mind, but that doesn't mean you need to text her the moment you open your eyes. Restrain yourself.

Don't answer the phone immediately when she calls. It's okay for it to go to voicemail sometimes.

Read books, go to counseling, and journal, but don't feel like you need to share every revelation with her. In fact, keep these to yourself. Let her see the change in your heart and ask.

Put Things on the Table Before You Pick Them Up

Chances are you've heard a lot of things from your wife about things you did wrong and why she has left. As a man willing to fix the marriage, your tendency is to pick up the things she says, own them, and jump into action.

Before doing so, you need to pause and evaluate her statements. Visualize putting her statement on the table. Don't pick it up yet. Is what she said true of you? If so, go ahead and pick it up; if not, leave it there. Maybe parts of it are true. Go ahead and pick up those parts, but leave the untrue parts behind.

As with other key aspects of this journey, go to God with it first. If you still have questions, ask your circle of trusted brothers. Then, pick up only those parts that you need to.

Psychologists talk about a powerful principle called "projection," which refers to the idea that we see in others what we most hate about ourselves. Think about the things that your wife has said are wrong with you:

- "You're not emotionally available."
- "You're too focused on your work."
- "I feel like I don't know you."
- "You don't care about me."

While these statements may have a seed of truth, the reality is that she may primarily be projecting things onto you that she hates about herself. In other words, perhaps she's not emotionally available, too fixated on her own issues, feels like she doesn't know herself, and doesn't care for who she is right now.

Sometimes we joke that women are the weaker sex. While that may be true physically, most men would concede that women are stronger when it comes to emotions and relationships. As a result, as men, we have a tendency to accept a woman's evaluation of a problem in a relationship. After all, she's got more emotional intelligence (EQ), right?

Add to her higher EQ the fact that she's lived with you a long time and has seen parts of you that nobody else has. This level of familiarity means that she has more insight on you than anyone else. So, we assume she's a source of good advice.

Right now, though, she is not a good source of advice. While women may have a higher EQ on average, and while she may know you better than anyone else, let's be honest about your current situation: your cheating wife's EQ just took a nosedive.

She's completely focused on herself, and distracted by the chemical rush of dopamine from new love and the flood of self-hatred. It's likely, therefore, that at least half of what she's trying to hang on you is her junk, not yours. Don't pick it up.

When she says something about you, don't just accept it as a fact. Put it on the table, consider it, and pray about it. Ask your friends or your counselor about it. If it's yours to pick up, own it and work on it. If not, leave it on the table.

I like the tip my friend's pastor gave him about bad advice. As a senior pastor, he hears all sorts of advice—some good, some very bad. He says when someone gives him bad advice or destructive input, he subtly tugs on his opposite ear lobe. "It's like I'm immediately flushing the toxic words out the other side of my head when I tug on my ear." While this might sound comical, small actions like this can be helpful.

Make a written list of everything she said about you since "D Day" (Discovery Day of her affair), or the day she informed you that she "needed some space." For the moment, just put these things on the table and analyze them.

Ask yourself: *What does this statement say about her?*

For example, if she says you're "not emotionally available," ask yourself, *Is she emotionally available? What about this is true of her?*

If there are things she says that you do want to pick up and own, that's okay. However, if you find that you're picking up and owning everything negative she says about you, alarm bells should go off. Ask yourself, *Is this mine to own?* I promise that at least half of what she's trying to hang on you needs to stay on the table. Flush all that out your ear!

Stop Enabling

Every addict needs people in their life who enable their habit. Addiction is typically a symbiotic relationship in that way. Your wife is addicted to the feelings she's getting from the affair. Her mind is consumed with how to arrange more time with the guy. Don't enable her addiction.

To spend time with her lover, she needs you to take care of the kids. Of course, she'd never come out and say, "Hey, can you watch the kids so I can spend time with my boyfriend?" Instead, she'll likely say: "Hey, I bet you've been missing the kids. Would you like to spend a little extra time with them?"

She may sprinkle in some guilt to kick it up to the next level: "Your kids have been asking about you. I know it's not your time until tomorrow, but why don't you go ahead and get them tonight."

Between wanting to win her back and being a good dad to your kids, you'll say, "Sure." However, what you're probably doing is enabling her habit. Every time you take the kids off her hands so she can go live in her fantasy world, you're relieving her of the responsibility of being a mom. You are also relieving her of the experience and heavy burden of what being a single mom will be like, should she choose to continue down her current path.

As much as your good self wants to say, "Sure, I'd love to see the kids," when it's her time to take care of them, do not relieve her of her parental responsibilities. This only enables her irresponsible behaviors.

Engage the Enemy

We've established the fact that there is a battle for your marriage and your family. If we lived in the Wild West, you could gather a posse and ride out to take care of the poor excuse of a man who is sleeping with your wife. If you did this, though, you would alienate her because she thinks she loves him.

So, what do you do? The battle must be fought on the spiritual plane. After all, the enemy behind all of this is Satan. He has orchestrated this, cheered it on, and is continually behind the scenes fueling it.

Your role as a warrior is to bring the Kingdom of God to this situation. As the leader of your home, you are both a priest and a king. As a priest, you have spiritual authority over your family. As a king, you have spiritual authority over your domain. You may have never realized this, but now it is high time to use that authority.

Declare Your Authority

The power behind that authority is from Jesus. So, when we take authority over the situation, we do it in his name. Since the authority we have is from the Kingdom of God, we bring everything under the command of the Kingdom.

As humans this side of heaven, I don't personally think we fully realize just how much power we have at our disposal. Think about it: the God who created the billions of planets and stars and put every fish and molecule of water in the seven seas is the same God under whose dominion you operate.

You might say something like this:

In the name of Jesus Christ, I take authority over my kingdom and domain. This is my marriage, my family, and my home. Right now, I bring all of it under the authority and reign of the Kingdom of God.

Saying these words out loud creates clarity. In the spiritual realm, you are stepping on the scene and taking charge. Remember, Satan and his demons are creatures—they can't read your thoughts or mind. By audibly declaring God's authority over your family and marriage, you are serving an eviction notice to the enemy. Then, let God do the rest.

Take Command

With your authority firmly established, now it is time to take command of the battle. To do this, we can again learn from David, one of the greatest warriors of all time.

One of the best things you can do is read the book of Psalms. There are several instances where David calls for the spiritual armies of the Kingdom to defeat his enemies. Use these verses as a model for your prayer. Here is a great example from Psalm 35:

O Lord, oppose those who oppose me. Fight those who fight against me.

Put on your armor, and take up your shield.

Prepare for battle, and come to my aid. Lift up your spear and javelin against those who pursue me. Let me hear you say,
"I will give you victory!"

In this Psalm, David begins by asking God to oppose those resist him. God is for you and for your marriage. He hates adultery and all of the foul spirits that are against your marriage.

David continues by asking God to fight for him. He does not hold back; neither should you.

Bring shame and disgrace on those trying to kill me;
turn them back and humiliate those who want to harm me.

Blow them away like chaff in the wind – a wind sent by the angel of the Lord.

Make their path dark and slippery,
with the angel of the Lord pursuing them.

I did them no wrong, but they laid a trap for me.
I did them no wrong, but they dug a pit to catch me.

So let sudden ruin come upon them!

Use this prayer against your true enemy: the demonic realm. Engage the armies of God to battle on your behalf. Then, rest in the peace and confidence of knowing that he is fighting for you:

Then I will rejoice in the Lord.
I will be glad because he rescues me.

With every bone in my body, I will praise him: "Lord, who can compare with you?

Who else rescues the helpless from the strong?

Who else protects the helpless and poor from those who rob them?"

Psalm 55 is another great example. Like you, David has been betrayed. At the end of the Psalm, he cries out to God to help him:

Cast your burden on the Lord and he will sustain you. He will never let the righteous be shaken. But you, O God, will bring them down to the pit of destruction. Blood thirsty, deceitful men will not live out half their days. But I will trust in you.

What's beautiful about the Psalms is that as you read them, not only will you find instructions for warfare, you'll also find healing for your broken heart.

Worship

This will be a tough battle with many twists and turns. On some days, the fog of war will settle in and you won't know which way is up. You'll feel physically and emotionally drained. It will take everything you have just to take another step forward.

Throughout history, the armies of God have gone into battle led by worship. You need to do the same.

Worship is whatever you give your heart to, expecting life in return. It is now be apparent that you have worshiped your wife—you gave your heart to her expecting to get the answers to your core questions, validating you as a man.

Worshiping God means coming before him and saying, "I give you my heart." In return, we look for him to bring us the life that we need.

Worship played a key role in carrying me through the darkest season of my life. Many nights after dinner, I found myself lying on my back on the floor of the living room, staring at the ceiling, worshiping God. At other times, I picked up my guitar and sang songs through tears.

In Psalm 51:17, David says, "The sacrifices of God are a broken spirit, a broken and contrite heart." Your heart is broken. Right now, it's time to worship. As I look back, these times of worship had an intensity not seen before or since.

Worship reorients your heart; it reminds you that God is real and is always with you. When the darkness closes in during the middle of a lonely night, or you awake and can't picture how you will make it through another day, or you get to the end of the day and you find yourself completely exhausted, you can worship him.

Worship will provide the strength you need for the battle. When it feels like you don't have anything left to give, you can draw on the strength of God.

Words of Encouragement

During the fight for my marriage, one of my good friends called me up and said she had a verse for me: "Your word is a lamp to my feet and a light to my path."[27] She reminded me that in the darkness, God will shine a light to show me the next step.

I am reminded again of a scene from *The Lord of the Rings*. In the second novel (and film), *The Two Towers*, Frodo and Sam walk in darkness as they enter the dark lair of Shelob, the giant spider. Sam reminds Frodo that he has in his possession the Phial of Galadriel, given to him as a gift by the elven queen Galadriel. Frodo uses the light of the phial to mark the way forward. For me, it's a powerful image of how God lights the way for us in dark places.

Currently, many things are unclear, and the future is uncertain. In this darkness, God will light your path. All you need to do is ask him about the next step. He will lead you.

In the familiar 23rd Psalm, David offers hope: "Though I walk through the valley of the shadow of death, I will fear no evil." Your journey has taken you into a dark valley. While I wish I could tell you that it will get easier soon, the reality is that you must walk through it.

While you are in this dark place, I want to encourage you with two things. First, you will eventually come out the other side. There will be brighter days ahead.

Second, God will light your path in this dark valley. Whenever you don't know the next step, which will be most of the time, turn to him in your heart and ask what you should do now. He will lead you. Because of this, you do not have to fear evil, for he is with you.

Finding Strength

I never felt more exhausted than during the season when my wife was cheating. Fighting for your heart, marriage, and family requires strength that you may not yet know you have. Pain and grief drain you emotionally.

Where do you get the energy to fight? How do you arrange your life during this crazy season? In this chapter, we'll share several practical things to help.

Give Your Heart Some Space

Be kind to your heart; it has taken a massive blow. Your wife's choices have deeply wounded you, and you're playing injured.

If you had a broken leg, you would expect it to hurt. You'd also give yourself some grace. You wouldn't expect to be able to go to the gym or run a 5K while it was healing.

Similar to a broken leg, you need to realize that your heart has been deeply wounded. You heart is literally broken. In the same way that you'd make some temporary changes to your activities for a broken leg, you need to make some accommodations to allow your heart to heal.

One way to do this is by getting into what I call your safe zone or "place of peace." For some men, it's the outdoors (the beach, mountains, desert). For others, it might mean going out with a friend to catch dinner and a movie. Get away from the pressure and reminders of your home right now. Even if it's just for a day, do the thing that really fills you up. It may seem crazy to "take a day off" when your life is in crisis, but that's exactly what I recommend.

Exercise Your Heart

Continuing with the metaphor of the broken leg, at some point the cast will come off and you have to do some physical therapy. If you don't do this, the muscles will atrophy and you'll lose the ability to walk.

Similarly, you need to exercise your heart. Just like the first steps in physical therapy are painful, this will be as well. This requires rebuilding your emotional strength. You can't repress the pain forever. If you do, you'll have long-term problems that will affect the rest of your life.

As I write this book, I've been going back to the gym. Weight training intentionally stretches and tears muscles with the intention of getting stronger. You know you're working out if you feel it the next day.

You know you're exercising your heart if you cause some level of intentional pain. In this season, one of the main emotions you will feel is grief. This is a deep sadness that comes following a loss. Expect to grieve.

Grief is processed through tears. Until now, you may not have cried very much as a man because you have been told that real men don't cry. Real men *do* cry. When there is pain, tears will be shed. You cannot experience the grief from being cheated on without a lot of tears. As you cry, though, reflect on how your life has changed and what has been lost.

Do this in small chunks. If you let grief pile up without being processed, it will cause problems. At some point, the festering wound will demand attention. It may be years from now, but when it does, you will implode and those around you will be hurt.

Physical therapy is necessary for someone with a broken leg. You may hate your physical therapist at the time. Later on, when you can walk, you'll be thankful for the pain they led you through.

Emotional therapy is necessary for someone with a broken heart. Just like you'd hire a physical therapist for your wounded leg, consider engaging a counselor to help you engage your heart. If you watched a person with a broken leg in the therapy room toughing it out while they learned to walk again, you'd respect them for enduring the pain. Similarly, you can hold yourself in high respect for going to see a counselor for your broken heart.

Beware, though, since most of us were taught not to cry, we probably are holding on to a lot of unprocessed grief from other things in our lives. When you open your heart up to grief, you may discover that there is a lot of pain and sadness buried inside.

In my life, I had suppressed things for decades. When I started processing the pain of my wife leaving me, I learned that there was much grief lurking deep in my heart. It too needed to be felt and cried through.

Don't be surprised if you discover a lot of ungrieved pain from other things in your past. As it surfaces, allow yourself to grieve. You're going to cry a lot, but it's not because you're falling apart; rather, you're coming back together—your broken heart is being made whole.

Don't be afraid to cry. David says that the Lord is near to the brokenhearted. Jesus says that he has come to bind up the brokenhearted (Isaiah 61:1). He will be right there with you in your grief.

You won't cry forever. The Psalmist says, "Though the sorrow may last for the night, His joy comes in the morning" (Psalm 30:5). If you grieve your loss and process your pain, there will come a day when you can move on.

Necessary Habits

During this crisis, your habits become more important than ever. We are the sum of our good habits; allow me to suggest some practical ones to help you navigate this season.

Exercise

The emotions swirling in your body need an outlet. Anger and sadness create a physical reaction. They take their toll on your body, draining you of energy needed to fight. Stress hormones like cortisol build up in your system, causing you to be lethargic and fueling depression.

Exercise helps you metabolize stress, anger, and grief. Find ways to exercise every day. Join a gym, or go for a walk. Play basketball, or mow the lawn. In addition to helping you process the stress, exercise gets you out of the house and around other people, which will lift your spirits.

Exercise also provides an outlet for the testosterone in your body. A pent-up sexual drive during this time of unchosen celibacy can lead you down dark paths that can do some serious damage to your life.

Shortly after my wife left, a storm blew a tree down in my backyard. This ended up being a lifesaver for me. When I felt sexual tension or anger, I'd head out to the backyard with a chainsaw and an axe. It's amazing what 30 minutes of chopping wood can do to release some energy.

Diet

Most men lose a lot of weight during this season because they don't eat. You may not be hungry, but you still need to eat. You need fuel to fight for your family.

Try to eat foods that will give you energy and keep you healthy. Resist the temptation to go to the drive-through every time. Instead, make a trip to the grocery store and buy some fruits and vegetables. Keep it simple. I try to remember this basic mantra: the closer it is to coming straight from the earth, air, sea, or stream, the healthier it is for you.

If you don't know how to cook, this is a great time to learn. You might find cooking to become a therapeutic hobby. After all, the majority of the world's great chefs are men.

Sleep

I had a hard time going to sleep alone. These quiet moments in bed at the end of the day, during the middle of the night, and waking up in the morning alone were brutal. Nothing was there to distract me from the heavy realities of my current situation.

I was tempted to binge-watch a TV series until the early hours of the morning so I would fall asleep in my recliner. There were many nights I didn't even go into the bedroom. Some nights, I slept on the couch. Other nights, I slept in the guest room.

You need sleep and rest to be able to live. You need to be clear-minded to make good decisions and love your kids. Yet, sleep can be hard to come by when your heart is crushed and your mind races through all of the "what if" scenarios.

How do you handle this? First, watch out for traps. Alcohol may knock you out, but you risk becoming addicted. Plus, while you may stagger to the bedroom and collapse, you don't sleep well and you wake up feeling terrible.

You might have a doctor prescribe sleeping pills. However, these can be addictive as well. Talk to your doctor about some healthy options.

Try to maintain good habits during this season. Eating well and exercising will help you sleep. Go to bed at the same time each night. Do the things you're supposed to do, like turn the lights down and the media off. This is a good time to pick up a book, especially if you're not a reader. A book can put you to sleep (hopefully not this one!), while also engaging your mind in something other than the current crisis.

Personally, I'd steer away from self-help type books at night because they get your mind thinking. Keep these for the morning. Instead, read novels. As a side benefit, a novel gives you a window into other people's lives.

Another way to sleep well is to get up earlier in the morning. Set an alarm 30 minutes or an hour before you normally get up. Take this time to read, journal, and pray.

When you wake up in the middle of the night, you need a strategy. These middle-of-the-night moments were the darkest, loneliest places of my life. This is when your mind can start racing and it can seem impossible to get back to sleep. If you're not someone who prays, this is a good time to start. Ask Jesus to come for you in your loneliness and pain.

Sometimes, I would pray in my bed. Other times, I'd get up and walk out onto my back porch. Feeling the cool night air while looking up at the stars somehow connected me to the reality that there was a world beyond my pain and a God who cared for me. After 15 minutes of that peace, I could usually go back to sleep.

Hobbies

If you're separated from your wife, you likely have some free time on your hands. Rather than sink into depression, pursue some hobbies. It's a great way to process stress.

When I was young, I loved to do anything that involved the outdoors and water. Hiking, camping, canoeing, and fishing played a big role in my childhood. As I became an adult, the demands of work and family crowded out these pursuits.

When my wife left, I decided to reconnect with the outdoors. I bought a pair of hiking boots, then I got on eBay and purchased a full set of backpacking gear. A friend of mine had started to get interested in sailing, so I went in 50% on an old sailboat. Fly fishing was always something I wanted to do, so I purchased the gear. I also pulled my acoustic guitar out of the closet, added some new strings, and began to play every day.

Over the next few months, these hobbies became my lifeline. Camping allowed me to get out in nature where I could breathe fresh air and process my feelings. On days when my wife had my son, I'd head up into the national forest and camp.

The sailboat became my place of solace. I spent many days floating around on our local lake, soaking in the sun, and letting the wind carry me. These became places where I could cry and yell. Getting in touch with my hobbies helped me reconnect with—and rediscover—who I was as an individual outside of married life.

Friends

While I was married, most of my social life revolved around other couples. Over the years with work and busyness, I'd lost regular connection with other guys. This season gave me the opportunity to build relationships with other men.

Here is some cautionary advice: this is not a good time to look for female friends. You're fighting for your marriage. If you start spending time with a woman and confide in her, you'll quickly find yourself in the same place as your wife. Remember, you are still married.

Many men look for a female friend to give them advice. It's easy to say, "She's just a friend", and it seems appealing to have the comfort and understanding of a female. Even if she has pure intentions, you risk giving her your hungry, vulnerable, and broken heart. This type of attachment will not be helpful as you are trying to sort things out and can be a dangerous trap.

Create a New Routine

Being married brings a natural rhythm to life. You wake up next to someone, you go to work, and then you come back together for the evening. Whatever that routine looked like in your marriage (healthy or unhealthy), it has now been disrupted.

In this season, you need to develop a new routine. If you don't do this proactively, you'll get sucked into bad habits.

Talk to most men and they'll tell you they are bored with their life. You now have the opportunity to redefine your schedule. While almost all of this season totally sucks, one of the benefits is being able to design your own life.

What does an ideal day look like to you in this period? Write down the things you'd like to do each day or during the week. Then, begin to build your schedule. Don't just leave your evenings and weekends blank.

It's okay to watch some TV or play some video games, but don't turn into a couch potato. Schedule time to work out and eat well. Get involved in a local sports league or your community. Schedule some recreation on the weekends. Reconnect with your hobbies or develop a new one.

Make time for church. I know it's hard to walk into a room full of seemingly happy families and sit by yourself. I challenge you to push through this. Even though not everyone will understand what you're going through, there are some who will. Plus, your kids will benefit from being at church.

One Sunday, I shook hands with a guy sitting behind me. Based on the two kids' jackets next to him, the lack of a ring on his finger, and the sad look in his eye, I could tell he was alone. We connected and started getting together. That divine encounter would not have happened if he had not taken the initiative and rose above his fear of sitting alone. I applaud him.

Developing a routine will help you keep your sanity. It may also have a side benefit. From the perspective of your wife, when she sees you getting along with your life and being healthy, she may be attracted to that. Whether she notices or not, though, you'll be laying the foundation for a good path forward in your life.

Keeping from Imploding

This may be the toughest season you will ever face in your life. Right now, if you can keep from imploding, you're doing well.

Counseling

You're not the first man to go through this, and unfortunately, you won't be the last. Trained counselors can help guide you through the process, helping you find some healing and sanity.

Having never been to counseling, I wasn't sure what to expect. The hour I spent with my counselor each week become something I looked forward to. She was able to ask questions that helped confirm I wasn't crazy. As I navigated through this period, my counselor helped me see things I could not

Let me be clear: counseling isn't fun. Working with your therapist has a lot of similarities with physical therapy. They will intentionally lead you to places of pain, challenging you to stretch yourself so you can heal.

Therefore, I recommend that you seek out a professional counselor. There is nothing wrong with getting advice from friends, older mentors, or pastors. While these folks all have good intentions, you will get much better results from a trained therapist. I know money is likely tight right now. Trust me—this is worth the investment. If insurance doesn't pay for it, squeeze it into your budget somehow; put it right up there in importance with the rent/mortgage and food budget. It's a temporary expense, most likely, but will pay long-term dividends.

Anti-Depressant Drugs

Much like my aversion to therapists, I thought anti-depressants were for other people. I never saw myself as a candidate to take these drugs.

The challenge was that I had become clinically depressed. More than likely, you are—or will become—depressed during this period. It's what a therapist or doctor would call "grief-onset depression." You don't have to be a PhD to know that the swirl of chemicals in your body may be dragging you down. Anti-depressants counteract the effects of these chemicals.

Thankfully, one of my good friends who is a nurse pulled me aside and told me that I really needed to see a doctor. My therapist was already telling me the same thing. It took some humility, but I went to my primary care physician and explained what I was going through. They prescribed a light dosage of a common anti-depressant. It was a lifesaver for me.

One helpful side effect of many anti-depressant drugs is that they tend to decrease your sex drive. I don't think I need to say much about how useful this can be if you're trying to fight for your marriage and not get pulled in harmful directions.

You don't have to take anti-depressants forever. Once you make it through this season, you can stop. Of course, you need to do all of this under the guidance of a doctor. The way that you taper off of drugs like these can be very important. Going cold turkey can be dangerous to your health and sanity.

After my life got back on plane, I weaned off the drugs. I haven't been depressed since then. If you're on the fence and your therapist recommends anti-depressants, I encourage you to take their advice.

There's no shame in taking medication for your current condition. Ask your doctor what's best for you. There are better days ahead. The more intentional you are in this season, the more prepared you will be to step into a better future.

Phase Four: Your Next Chapter

You've been through a dark valley, sought healing for your heart, and fought for your marriage. Now, it's time to emerge on the other side as a stronger man.

It's time to write the next chapter of your life. Your future still hangs in the balance. While you have no guarantees, what you do have is a stronger, more healed version of yourself.

Every man's story is different. Some men reading this book have the opportunity to return to their marriage; others find themselves divorced. In either case, you must care for the children and learn to forgive your wife.

Wherever you find yourself, the next chapter of your life will involve rebuilding from the ashes. It will take strength and hard work. It seems like you deserve some rest. While that may be true, now more than ever is a critical time to man up and press in.

Loving Your Children

Whether or not they understand what is happening, your children are involved. As their father, your role is to love them at a time when you have so little to give. In this chapter, you'll discover both inspiration and practical ideas on how to care for the children during this crisis.

What She Will Do

Part of what may have driven your wife from her family was a feeling of being trapped in her role as a mother.

A huge lie of the enemy that your wife may have accepted is that the children will be okay. He's assured her that other children have gone through this and that it's not that big of a deal. Just as she is deceived with the affair, she is similarly deceived when it comes to its effects on the children.

At the same time, chances are she feels a lot of guilt and shame for how her choices pulled her away from her children. She loves them. So, while she is running away and giving huge amounts of her heart to her lover, she feels a tremendous burden for even wanting to escape from her role as a mom. This compounds the regular level of guilt that most moms carry as they hear the inner voice say, *You're not doing enough for your kids.*

This guilt will flow into her mothering. When you put yourself in her situation, you see that there are two probable responses: supermom and absent mom. It's likely she'll bounce back and forth between the two. Let's examine these.

Supermom

During an affair, many women go into supermom mode. Since they feel guilty for neglecting their kids, they want to prove to everyone that they are a good mom. They also need to show that they can be a good *single* mom.

So, they work hard to overcompensate. Supermoms can manifest in many ways, such as when they:

- Buy the kids whatever they want

- Become lax in discipline
- Go out of their way to spend time with them

As the dad, this can be very frustrating. While you're doing your best just to hold it together in front of your kids, she's working to receive the "mom-of-the-year" award. While you're trying to figure out how to pay the bills, she's running up the credit card buying your kids the toys and shoes they want. While you're trying to maintain some kind of discipline and normalcy, she's loosened the restrictions.

This dynamic has all kinds of challenges. Maybe you want to look like a good dad to your kids, so parenting becomes a competition. If she buys them one video game, you buy them two. If she takes them to Six Flags, you take them to Disneyland. There is no good end to this competition. You're likely already stretched financially. Plus, your kids will learn to play off your emotions and take advantage of you. In the process, they'll become spoiled.

A friend told me a story about a family down the street that was going through a divorce. The young teenage son was seen riding a brand-new bike through the neighborhood. When my friend's son asked him about it, the kid with the new bike said, "It's a guilt offering from my Dad. I can get anything I want out of my parents right now."

Keep in mind, though, that the opposite response can also be dangerous. She's buying them whatever they want and loosening the rules, so you become more restrictive. She's spending all of the money, so you don't spend any. Even worse, you become resentful and this hurts your kids.

Since you cannot control her choices, what do you do?

Don't get sucked into the trap. This is going to require a lot of grace on your part. Yes, you need to take care of your kids' basic needs. However, do it in a way that is consistent with what they experienced before all of this happened. Just as you shouldn't whip out your credit card to compete with her overspending on the kids, neither should you tighten up your spending to offset her expenses.

The same thing goes for the rules. Her moral compass is out of whack. Yes, she's probably going to be much more permissive than she was before. That doesn't mean you should relax your rules. It also doesn't mean you need to overcompensate by tightening them. The best thing you can do is maintain an environment that is consistent with what your children experienced before she cheated.

Absent Mom

While some women become supermoms during this chaotic time of separation, others become absent moms. Maybe she leaves and is no longer around the children. Maybe she is so consumed with the affair that she doesn't have any emotional energy to offer, or is so overcome with shame that she can't bear to be with her kids. Maybe she is hungover from the substance abuse used to numb that pain.

As much as you long for her presence in your daily life, you need to know that your kids are deeply hurt by their mom's absence. They miss her. While they love you, every child needs their mom.

In the middle of this, children have all kinds of questions. Why did she leave? Where is she? Will she come back? The answers they determine get filtered through their young perspective with limited experience.

The most common, often-unspoken question a child has is, "What did I do to cause this?" The enemy will whisper to them that they were the reason she left. Then, they will be consumed with trying to figure out what they did wrong.

Your role is to let your children know it's not their fault. It begins with prayer. Ask the Father to protect them from the lies of the enemy and to heal their broken hearts. Ask him to give you wisdom to cooperate with this process.

How to Be Consistent

As much as supermom may be trying to win their hearts with spending and lax rules, what the kids really crave is consistency. Therefore, try as much as possible to maintain some normalcy with their schedule. Do the usual things: cook dinner, watch TV together, and help them with their homework.

Maintain Their Current Living Arrangements

If possible, try not to disrupt their living arrangements. If you can keep the house, do so. Remember, she's the one who is walking away from the marriage, so if she wants to go, it's her that leaves the house, not you.

If she eventually leaves on a semi-permanent or permanent basis, perhaps you and your estranged wife can take turns living with the kids in your existing home (even if your wife is keeping a second apartment). This way, the kids don't have to schlep between your place and your wife's, and they always get to sleep in their own beds.

The other advantage with parents being the ones who come and go, rather than the kids, is if your wife is living with her new lover. This way, the kids don't have to sleep under the same roof as the other guy. As well, if they stay in their current home, you can continue to pray through the house and maintain Christ's authority as the Landlord over the property.

Be Loving

More than new toys and fewer rules, what your children crave is love. The problem is that you feel a lot of anger, so it's easy for this to affect your kids.

Look, on any given day, kids can be annoying and cause anger to rise up. Now it's worse. You have to parent your kids on your own. This means you are the only one to respond to their needs. In a time when you don't have much energy, it's easy to have a short fuse.

Imagine having an absent mom and an angry dad. I know you don't want this for your children. Your children can't be an outlet for your anger. They need your love. They need grace.

One way to keep from letting your anger spill out on them is to remember that they're in the same boat with you. She cheated on you, but her actions have also impacted your children. Even if you are not separated, they can sense something is wrong. Seeing your children in the same situation as you can help turn anger to compassion.

As well, you need a safe outlet when you feel like your fuse is getting short. Call one of your trusted brothers and let him know what's going on. Lean on your friends right now; they care and want to be there for you (just as they know you would be there for them if the situation were reversed).

Be Appropriately Sad

As much as you are struggling with sadness, the kids too are sad. While they may still see their mom, she is gone for huge chunks of the time. The stability that they enjoyed in having a family has been removed.

One tendency is to try to keep it all together for the kids. If they are going to be sad, you want to stiffen up, not let them see your emotion, and tell them everything will be okay. This leaves them feeling alone in their sadness.

Another option is to let your children see all of your sadness. However, if you completely fall apart in front of them, this can leave them feeling even more disoriented and insecure. It will cause them to stiffen up as they realize that if you can't hold it together, they are going to need to.

Somewhere in the middle of these two extremes, you need to demonstrate an appropriate level of sadness to your kids. It's okay if they get a window into your broken heart. They need to know that it's fine and appropriate to be sad and to cry.

Find the Energy to Parent

Where do you get the energy to parent? Your role right now is to love them. However, you've been sapped of all your emotional energy. How are you supposed to invest in your kids while you are so drained?

This is why you desperately need to lean into your relationship with God. When you have no physical or emotional energy, go to him. He loves you and your kids. Ask him to fill you up.

What brings you energy? It's usually a combination of physical and spiritual activity. For the children, find activities that can allow them to diffuse some of their emotional stress. Go for a walk or a hike; go to the park; throw a baseball. These allow all of you to blow off some steam while providing something for you to do together.

Your kids also need proper nutrition. You don't have to be Emeril Lagasse or Julia Child to cook a healthy dinner. Take some time to make a nutritious meal for you and your kids. Then, sit around the table together. This is normalcy for them, and it helps bring them energy.

Fight for Them

What would you do if an armed invader broke into your home and threatened your children? Like every man, something in you would rise up to defend your family and fight for them. You would take a bullet for them.

This situation is no different. You have an enemy invading your home, threatening your children. The challenge is that you can't see him; you can only see his effects.

How do you fight this enemy? You fight in prayer. As the father, you have authority over your family. You might say, "In the name and authority of Jesus, as the head of this house, I take full authority over my children."

Next, I recommend that you bring your children under the authority and protection of the Kingdom of God. You might say, "I bring my children under the full authority of the Kingdom of God with all of its power, protection, provision, and healing."

In his book, *Moving Mountains,* John Eldredge calls this process "consecration." You intentionally align everything with the Kingdom of God. In the case of your children, this will be tremendously helpful.

Next, you intercede for them. To intercede means to stand in the gap for someone who may not be able to pray for themselves. Your children may be too young to pray for themselves—not in the way that you can. Right now, they need more than sweet bedtime prayers.

Thus, pray for their hearts to be protected. Ask for their healing, and pray against the spirits of fear and abandonment. Ask God to protect them.

Some of these may be prayers of passion and righteous anger. As such, I don't recommend you say them in front of your children. It will only scare them. When you pray with your children, be much more tender, but don't forget to also pray behind the scenes. In these prayers, you can be as forceful as any father would be toward someone invading his home.

The best times for these prayers are after you drop your children off at their mom's. They need your intercession. When you drop them off, smile and tell them you love them. Then, as you drive away, begin praying aggressively for their hearts and against their enemy.

Answering the Hard Questions

Your children will have hard questions—many of which will not have good answers. This can be very frustrating.

First, have compassion for your children. Their family is falling apart. Their mom and dad have serious issues. They want to know what's going on and they want to help, so be patient with them. Their hearts are breaking just as yours is.

As you search to answer their questions, reassure them that it is not their fault. Most children think they had a role to play. Therefore, they believe they need to help fix the problem. The more you can reassure them that it is not their fault, the less of a burden they feel to have to solve the problem.

Your answers should not dishonor their mother. Resist the temptation to accuse her and justify yourself. It will not help to say things like, "Your mom left us because she is acting like an irresponsible teenager and doesn't care about our family."

Instead of accusation and judgement, show your children some of your sadness. Here's a suggestion for achieving an appropriate level of shared sadness: imagine that your children are acquaintances, such as a casual friend or a co-worker. There's a time and place to share with such people that you are estranged from your wife, that it is a hard, sad time, but you are confident that you will get through it. Think about taking such a balanced—but not overly emotional—approach with your children.

The answers need to also be as honest as possible. Don't sugar coat the situation or make promises you can't keep. Telling your children that everything will be all right or that you and their mom will work things out is not an honest answer. The outcome is not assured.

One of the best things you can do is to end your answers with a question to them. It may help stop a long string of awkward questions that you can't really answer, and it will give you an opportunity to ask about their heart.

When they ask why she left, you might say: "Your mom and I have some things to work out and she left to have some time to think about them. I know you're sad. I'm sad too. I want you to know that in all of this, we both love you very much. How are you feeling?"

When they ask what's going to happen, you might say: "I'm not sure exactly what is going to happen. As I know, I'll tell you. I do want you to know that in all of this, I love you very much. So does your mom. That will never change. How are you doing with all of this today?"

Your wife will likely get these same questions. Sadly, many of her answers may be unfair to you. In her attempt to justify her actions, she might accuse you of things that aren't completely true. When these accusations get back to you, it can be easy to lose your cool. I recommend that you do everything in your power to stay calm.

When your child says, "Dad, mom said that you did this," take a deep breath. Then, as calmly as you can, say something like: "Right now, your mother and I see things differently. We're working on that. In all of this, I want you to know that I love you and that I'm praying for you every day."

If they keep pressing you with questions that you can't really answer, you can redirect the conversation. Once again, do your best to be patient. After all, haven't you been pressing your wife to answer questions? And aren't you unsatisfied with the answers? There just simply aren't good answers to all of the questions. The important thing is that your children know you love them, that it's not their fault, and that you are going to be there for them.

Behind the scenes, you need to pray. As you do, ask God to give you wisdom, calm their curious minds, and heal their broken hearts. Above all, love your children with tenderness, compassion, and patience. They need all of the affection you can muster.

This very well could be the most difficult time of your entire life. By navigating it with balance, dignity, and wisdom, while still fighting a warrior's fight for the heart of your family, you will be setting a powerful example for your children. The seeds you sow by handling this as a man of God, surrendered to his will and plan, will pay dividends in your children's lives—and even their children's lives.

I encourage you to meditate on the powerful words of Psalm 1 (1-3):

Blessed is the man who walks not in the counsel of the ungodly, nor stands in the path of sinners, nor sits in the seat of the scornful; but his delight is in the law of the Lord, and in His law, he meditates day and night. He shall be like a tree planted by the rivers of water, that brings forth its fruit in its season, whose leaf also shall not wither; and whatever he does shall prosper.

Many children have been through the separation and divorce of their parents. There are few things harder for a child to endure. Your role is to love them in the middle of it.

As you grapple with the current crisis, pray that God will help you keep your eye on the end goal: to honor, love, and raise your children the best way you know how. He will give you resources and capacity you did not know you had. As you commit your children to him, he will indeed plant your tree (you and your family) by the rivers of his living water.

Forgiveness

Whether you are reconciling with your wife or headed to divorce court, you must deal with forgiveness. It has been said that unforgiveness is like drinking poison and expecting the other person to die. Harboring bitterness and unforgiveness toward your wife will kill you.

Naturally, you have a reason to be angry toward your wife. However, you need to realize the cost of unforgiveness will exact a heavy toll on you and your kids.

How do you forgive her? After all, she has ruined your life. Her actions have destroyed your family. She's dealt a crushing blow to your masculinity, and she's hurt your children. Because of her, you're likely in financial ruins. Most of all, she's smashed your heart. You wonder if you'll ever be able to trust a woman again.

Living in unforgiveness is dangerous because it allows the enemy a stronghold in your life. Paul tells us not to let the sun go down on our anger, "for anger gives a foothold to the devil." (Ephesians 4:26-27) After the season you went through, you've likely been angry for a long time. If you keep living like this, you risk giving the enemy free reign to wreak havoc on your life.

I was able to see this in my life. After I got divorced, I looked good on the outside, but inside I was consumed with bitterness.

One weekend, I got a clear picture of the access I was giving the enemy. About 18 months after my divorce, I was leading a session at a men's retreat. Before, during, and after the session, I had a group of men praying for me. I had never been more spiritually covered in my life.

That night, I went to sleep. All night long, I was tortured with dark dreams that I can only describe as "pure evil." Never before or since have I experienced dreams that awful.

Finally, at about 4:30 that morning, I gave up on trying to sleep. I got out of bed, threw on some clothes, and walked down to the river near the facility where I was staying. Next to the river, I cried out to God in my frustration. "What is up with these demonic dreams? I just spent the evening serving you, and I had all of these guys praying for me. What happened?"

In the darkness next to the stream, I heard the voice of the Father. He said, "You need to forgive her." At that moment, it all became clear. I had been holding onto unforgiveness. Despite my friends' prayers, the anger in my heart had given access to my enemy.

In that moment, I fell to my knees. Tears streamed down my face as I choked out the words, "I forgive her." The darkness lifted.

Forgiveness is impossible on your own. However, in Jesus, forgiveness is not only possible, it is required.

We don't forgive out of our feelings. We forgive out of our faith. Forgiving your ex-wife can only be done in Jesus. You might say something like: "In the name of Jesus and because of his sacrifice, I forgive her."

It was at this point that I truly began to understand the sacrifice of Jesus. Having to forgive someone who had so deeply wronged me brought me a deep understanding of God's grace.

Several months later, I was walking in the woods when I heard the voice of God say words that challenged me even more. He said, "You need to forgive him." Forgiving my wife was difficult, but she was someone that I had loved. Forgiving the man that slept with my wife and did irreparable damage to my family was much harder. I had never felt any love or compassion for that person. Yet, I knew that I needed to forgive him as well, or else the poison of bitterness would consume me.

You need to forgive. Otherwise, you'll carry around a poison that will consume you. It will dominate your thoughts, make you an angry person, and allow access to the enemy.

Forgiveness does not excuse or minimize what your wife did. Forgiveness takes the full weight and impact of the offense and brings it to Jesus. Remember, he bore the entire burden of all the sins of the world on the cross.

However, just because you forgive her does not mean that you now need to trust her. Forgiveness is given; trust is earned. If trust is to be regained, it will happen over time.

You don't necessarily need to tell her that you have forgiven her. Walk with God in this. When I first found out my wife was cheating, in my desperation to get her back, I declared my forgiveness. She wasn't really looking for forgiveness at that time, as she didn't think she was wrong. Furthermore, my offer was likely interpreted as a green light to continue what she was doing.

Instead of just telling her, consider genuinely forgiving her and then living it out. Be kind to her, don't hold grudges, and let her see the fruits of forgiveness. Remember, forgiveness is for your benefit first. If she responds, that's a bonus.

In the blood of Jesus, you can forgive. If you're like me, you'll need to do this many times. I think this is why Jesus told his disciples that they didn't need to forgive seven times, but seventy times seven. I'm sure I've forgiven my wife at least 490 times. Even a decade later, when something triggers anger in my heart toward her, I say, "Jesus, I forgive her."

As I forgave my unfaithful wife, something amazing happened in my heart. In that moment, I began to glimpse how much I had been forgiven. Just as my wife was unfaithful to me, I had been unfaithful to God. I had broken his heart. Yet, he chose to forgive me. The magnitude of this was overwhelming. For the first time in my life, I began to see the beauty and the cost of the forgiveness that Jesus freely extends through his sacrifice.

If you think about it, Jesus has forgiven her. All he is asking you to do is cooperate with him.

The ability to forgive is the gift of God to you. Along with forgiveness, you'll find freedom as the poison of bitterness is drained from your heart. Take advantage of it—forgiveness was Jesus's gift to you. Forgiving her is your gift back to him.

What Now?

Recovering from your wife's affair is a journey. There will be twists and turns. There will be many low points. However, as you intentionally cooperate with the Lord, he will lead you through this valley and out the other side.

I don't know your story and I don't know your future. You may end up reunited with your current wife. You may find yourself divorced.

It may not feel like it right now, but there are better days ahead. The way you handle this season will prepare you for this future. My prayer is that you will take the ideas in this book and put them to work. Walk with God through the valley and there will be better days ahead.

Resources

For more resources to help you on your journey, visit *www.shecheated.com*.

www.ingramcontent.com/pod-product-compliance
Lightning Source LLC
Chambersburg PA
CBHW052038090426
42739CB00010B/1962

* 9 7 8 1 7 3 7 0 7 6 1 0 0 *